CHEMISTRY IN CONTEXT

LABORATORY MANUAL

GRAHAM HILL AND JOHN HOLMAN

FIFTH EDITION

UNIVERSITY OF
BEDFORDSHIRE

D0237639

Text © John Holman, Graham Hill 1982, 1989, 1995, 2001
Original illustrations © Nelson Thornes Ltd 2001.

The right of John Holman & Graham Hill to be identified as authors of this work has been asserted by them in accordance with the Copyright, Designs and Patents Act 1988.

All rights reserved. No part of this publication may be reproduced or transmitted in any form or by any means, electronic or mechanical, including photocopy, recording or any information storage and retrieval system, without permission in writing from the publisher or under licence from the Copyright Licensing Agency Limited, of Saffron House, 6-10 Kirby Street, London EC1N 8TS.

Any person who commits any unauthorised act in relation to this publication may be liable to criminal prosecution and civil claims for damages.

First published in 1982 by:
Thomas Nelson and Sons Ltd

Fifth Edition published in 2001 by:
Nelson Thornes (Publishers) Ltd
Delta Place
27 Bath Road
CHELTENHAM
GL53 7TH
United Kingdom

08 /14 13 12 11 10 9 8 7 6

A catalogue record for this book is available from the British Library

ISBN 978 0 17 448307 6

Page make-up by Mathematical Composition Setters Ltd
Printed and bound in Slovenia by Delo tiskarna
by arrangement with Korotan-Ljubljana

UNIVERSITY of
BEDFORDSHIRE

Contents

Section 1: Practicals

Section 2: Investigations

Introduction

This Fifth Edition of the *Laboratory Manual* has been planned as a companion to the Fifth Edition of *Chemistry in Context* and as a response to the introduction of Advanced Subsidiary (AS) GCE alongside Advanced (A) GCE Courses.

The *Laboratory Manual* is totally self contained and can be used independently of the main text.

The book is divided into two main sections comprising:

Practicals and Investigations

The style and presentation of both the Practicals and the Investigations have been fully revised from the previous edition to achieve a smoother transition from GCSE and to cater for all students studying for AS level. A number of practicals and investigations in the previous edition have been replaced by more appropriate experimental and investigative work for the new specifications.

Section 1: Practicals

Each practical is self-contained and designed to introduce or develop a major area of chemistry. The Practicals include detailed instructions, a full list of Requirements and an approximate time allocation. Most of them are designed to occupy about 1 hour of practical work.

The Practicals also include questions designed to help students think about what they are doing rather than performing instructions mechanically.

Section 2: Investigations

This section provides suggestions and starting points for students to carry out their own open-ended investigations. The Investigations contain no detailed instructions, the intention being for students to plan their own experimental procedures.

Students will, of course, need to discuss possible plans with their teacher, who will need to check safety in particular before students start any experimental work.

The full list of Investigations has been divided into shorter investigations requiring about 3 or 4 hours of experimental work and longer investigations requiring about 10–12 hours.

Further guidance on the approach to and implementation of the Investigations is available at *www.chemistry-in-context.co.uk*.

Opportunities to assess practical skills

All of the AS and A level specifications require students to develop their practical and investigative skills of planning, implementing, analysing, concluding and evaluating.

The development and assessment of these skills can be made using most of the practicals in Section 1 and a grid is included after this introduction which maps the various skills to be assessed against the different practicals.

Nomenclature, units and abbreviations

Throughout the *Laboratory Manual*, we have used the International System of Units (SI) and nomenclature, following recommendations in *Signs, Symbols and Systematics* published by the Association for Science Education in 2000.

Safety

In planning and writing the experimental and investigative work for both the practicals and the investigations, safety considerations have been given the highest priority. We are particularly grateful for the helpful and experienced guidance of Peter Borrows, Past Chairman of the Safeguards in Science Committee of the Association for Science Education.

In **Section 1 (Practicals)**, hazardous substances and operations are identified and indicated by standard symbols, and appropriate precautions are recommended. Nevertheless, teachers should be aware of their responsibilities under the Health and Safety at Work Act, the Control of Substances Hazardous to Health (COSHH) Regulations and the Management of Health and Safety at Work Regulations. In this respect, teachers should follow the requirements of their employers at all times.

In **Section 2 (Investigations)**, students should carry out their own risk assessments, identifying hazards and suitable procedures for reducing the risks from them. Teachers must, however, check their students' risk assessments before experimental work begins, to ensure they meet their responsibilities as described in the previous paragraph.

More detailed information on safety for students is given on pages ix to xi. Additional safety guidance for carrying out Investigations is given on pages 136 to 137.

Once again, we are greatly indebted to our publishers for their efficient and professional translation of our original text into an attractive book. We would also like to thank Derek Denby of John Leggott College, Scunthorpe for his valuable help with the Investigations.

Finally, we thank our wives, Elizabeth and Wendy, for their continued support and encouragement.

Graham Hill
John Holman

November 2000

Opportunities for the Assessment of Practical Skills

All of the Advanced Subsidiary GCE and Advanced GCE Specifications in Chemistry introduced in September 2000 are based on the Subject Criteria for Chemistry. These criteria require students to develop their practical and investigative skills in order to:

- plan experimental activity   i.e. **planning**
- carry out experimental work   i.e. **implementing**
- analyse and draw conclusions from the results of their experimental work   i.e. **analysing and concluding**
- evaluate their work   i.e. **evaluating**

An assessment of these practical and investigative skills can be made using separate practical activities. Many of the experiments and activities in this book lend themselves well to the development, practice and assessment of practical and investigative skills.

In table 1, overleaf, specific practicals are mapped against the experimental skills which they could be used to assess.

Note:

a In some specifications, 'implementing' includes both carrying out experiments and recording observations and measurements, while in other specifications, carrying out and recording are assessed separately.

b In some specifications, analysing, concluding and evaluating are assessed under the same heading.

Practical	Practical number	Planning	Implementing	Analysing and Concluding	Evaluating
Analysing aspirin tablets	2	✓	✓	✓	✓
Analysing iron tablets	3	✓	✓	✓	✓
Determining the percentage of copper in brass	4	✓	✓	✓	✓
Studying redox reactions	5		✓	✓	
Enthalpy changes of neutralisation	7			✓	✓
Determining the enthalpy change for the thermal decomposition of KHCO$_3$	8	✓		✓	✓
Electrochemical cells	11	✓			
Complex formation and competition for cations	12		✓	✓	
Determining the formulae of complex ions	13	✓	✓	✓	
Determining the equilibrium constant for an esterification reaction	14			✓	✓
Determining the order of a reaction	15	✓		✓	✓
Using colorimetry to find the order of the reaction between bromine and methanoic acid	17			✓	
Determining the activation energy of the reaction between Br$^-$ and BrO$_3^-$ ions	18	✓	✓	✓	✓
Copper and copper compounds	23		✓	✓	
Alkenes	26		✓		
Aromatic compounds	27		✓		
1-Bromobutane	28		✓		
Nucleophilic substitution reactions of halogenoalkanes	29	✓			
Phenol	31		✓		
Carboxylic acids	33			✓	
Amines	34			✓	

Table 1
Opportunities for assessment

Safety in the Chemistry Laboratory

It is your duty in law to take reasonable care for your own health and safety, and that of others working in the laboratory. Safety is largely a matter of common sense, provided you know the hazards associated with the chemicals and procedures you are using. A **hazard** is anything with the potential to cause harm, for example, some chemicals and some activities such as heating. A **risk** is the likelihood of harm actually being caused by a hazard. This depends on the chance of something going wrong, the seriousness of any injury and the number of people who might be affected.

Table 1 lists the chemical hazards in substances you are likely to meet and the symbols used for these hazards. It is sensible, however, to regard **all** chemicals as potentially hazardous.

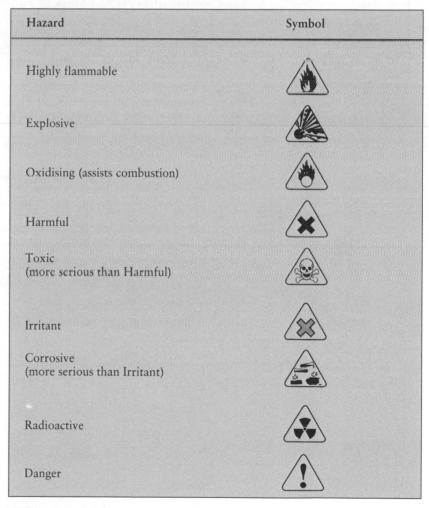

Hazard	Symbol
Highly flammable	
Explosive	
Oxidising (assists combustion)	
Harmful	
Toxic (more serious than Harmful)	
Irritant	
Corrosive (more serious than Irritant)	
Radioactive	
Danger	

Table 1
Chemical hazards

Risk assessments

A risk assessment identifies all the hazards associated with the chemicals you will be using, those you will be making and the procedures that you follow. It then requires a consideration of how likely it would be for that hazard to cause harm, and how serious that harm would be. It then gives ways to reduce the risks from these hazards and lists the safety precautions (control measures) to be taken.

For the Practicals in Section 1, we have shown the hazards and the safety precautions you should take. **To alert you to the more hazardous materials and operations, we have printed CARE in capitals and bold type followed by specific warnings in italic.**

For the Investigations in Section 2, it is not possible to identify the hazards until you have planned what you will do in your investigation. You will therefore need to carry out your own risk assessment as part of planning your investigation, and discuss it with your teacher before you start work. The general guidance on Investigations on pages 136 to 137 shows you how to carry out a risk assessment.

Some important points to remember

Always wear eye or face protection when carrying out practical work. Eye protection should be worn by *everyone* when anyone in the laboratory is doing practical work.

Always handle highly flammable liquids, such as ethanol and propanone, with great care and keep them away from naked flames. Heat test tubes of highly flammable liquids by immersing them in a beaker of hot water, taken from a hot tap or electric kettle, as shown in figure 1.

Always use a boiling tube when heating a non-flammable liquid over a bunsen flame and shake very gently during heating as shown in figure 2. Do not fill the tube more than one-fifth full.

Never point a test tube containing chemicals which you are heating towards yourself or anyone else. Do not fill tubes more than one-fifth full of the substance you are heating, as shown in figure 3.

Always report accidents, spills and breakages, however small, to your teacher.

Always make sure chemicals are labelled, and check the name and concentration on the bottle is *exactly* that of the chemical you require. Label clearly any chemicals you are keeping for future use. (Pour liquids from bottles away from the label side, so that drips do not damage the label.)

Always work steadily and without undue haste.

Always pipette liquids with a safety filler.

Always wear a laboratory coat whenever possible. Make sure it is fastened, not flapping open. Do not allow ties or scarves to hang loosely.

Always wash your hands after practical work.

Never put your head or clothes near a bunsen flame. Long hair should be tied back. Some hair preparations (e.g. wet-look gels) make the hair more flammable than usual and should be avoided. Adjust the bunsen to give a luminous flame when you are not using it.

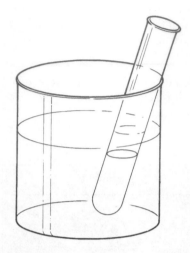

Figure 1
Flammable liquids should be heated in a beaker of hot water with no naked flames nearby.

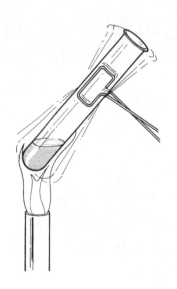

Figure 2
Non-flammable liquids should be heated in a boiling tube not more than one-fifth full, with gentle shaking.

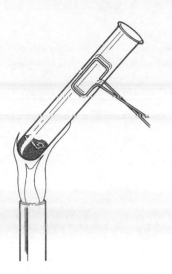

Figure 3
Solids should be heated in a tube not more than one-fifth full, and not pointing at anyone.

Never wear open-toed sandals in the laboratory. Your footwear should give some protection to your feet.

Never smell gases directly – only very cautiously, and with your lungs already filled with air. Waft the fumes gently towards your nose as shown in figure 4. If you are asthmatic, make sure your teacher is aware of this.

Never put your thumb or finger over the end of a test tube when shaking. Stopper the tube with a cork or bung.

Never try to force glass tubing when putting it into, or removing it from, corks or bungs. Always hold glass tubing in a cloth when performing these operations.

Never hold bottles by the neck. If a stopper is tight, get help. Do not try to force it off. Always pour liquids from the label side, so drips do not damage the label.

Never remove chemicals or equipment from the laboratory.

Never do practical work alone. If your teacher allows you to do practical work outside school hours, make sure somebody is within earshot.

Never perform unauthorised experiments. If you are asked to design or plan an investigation, always get it approved by your teacher before carrying it out.

Never taste anything unless you are instructed to do so.

Never eat, drink or apply cosmetics in the laboratory.

Figure 4
Smelling a gas safely. Cautiously waft the fumes towards your nose, with your lungs full of air.

Finding the formula of Epsom salts

REQUIREMENTS

Each student will need:

Eye protection

Rack and one clean, dry, hard-glass test tube

Solid hydrated magnesium sulphate (Epsom salts)

(approx. 2–3 g)

Spatula

Bunsen burner

Test tube holder

Access to balance

Time required   45 minutes

Introduction

Epsom salts are hydrated magnesium sulphate. Their formula is sometimes written as $MgSO_4.xH_2O$. In this experiment, you will be trying to find the value of x (i.e. the number of moles of water associated with one mole of $MgSO_4$ in Epsom salts).

Principle

When Epsom salts are heated, their water of crystallisation is driven off, leaving anhydrous magnesium sulphate, $MgSO_4$.

$$MgSO_4.xH_2O(s) \rightarrow MgSO_4(s) + xH_2O(g)$$

By weighing the hydrated and anhydrous magnesium sulphate before and after heating, it is possible to find the mass of $MgSO_4$ and the mass of H_2O in a sample of Epsom salts. From these masses, you can calculate the number of moles of water associated with one mole of $MgSO_4$. You can then write the precise formula for Epsom salts.

Procedure

EYE PROTECTION MUST BE WORN

CARE!
Eye protection must be worn.

Weigh a clean, dry test tube.

Put about 1 cm depth of Epsom salts in the test tube and reweigh.

Record these weighings and those which follow in a clear table.

Now, heat the test tube gently for a minute and then strongly for 5 minutes. Allow the tube to cool and then reweigh it.

1   What do you understand by the terms:
    a hydrated,   **b** anhydrous,   **c** water of crystallisation?

2   Describe what happens as the Epsom salts are heated.

3   How could you show that water is given off when Epsom salts are heated?

Heat the tube again for 2 minutes. Allow it to cool and reweigh. If the last two weighings differ by more than 0.05 g, repeat the heating and weighing again. This heating of a substance, like Epsom salts, until its weight does not change any more is called 'heating to constant weight'.

4 Why must the Epsom salts be heated to constant weight?

5 From your results table, find by subtraction of the appropriate weighings:

   a the mass of hydrated $MgSO_4$ you used,
   b the mass of water in this hydrated salt,
   c the mass of $MgSO_4$ in this hydrated salt.

6 Calculate the relative formula mass of:
   a water (H_2O),   b magnesium sulphate ($MgSO_4$).
      ($H = 1$, $O = 16$, $Mg = 24$, $S = 32$)

7 Rewrite the sentences below, filling in the missing data.

   From my results:
   ___ g of H_2O combine with ___ g of anhydrous $MgSO_4$ in Epsom salts
   ⇒ ___ moles of H_2O combine with ___ moles of anhydrous $MgSO_4$ in Epsom salts
   ⇒ ___ moles of H_2O combine with 1 mole of anhydrous $MgSO_4$.

8 Write a precise formula for Epsom salts.

Practical 2

Analysing aspirin tablets

REQUIREMENTS

Each pair of students will need:

Eye protection

Aspirin tablets (about 5)

Pipette (25 cm³) and safety filler

Burette and stand

Small beaker

2 standard flasks (250 cm³) (one for each partner)

Conical flask (250 cm³)

Small funnel

Bunsen burner

Tripod and gauze

Approximately 1.0 mol dm⁻³ sodium hydroxide solution (**corrosive**) (30 cm³), 0.10 mol dm⁻³ hydrochloric acid (150 cm³), phenol red (or phenolphthalein) indicator (**highly flammable solution**)

Time required $1\frac{1}{4}$ hours

Introduction

Aspirin is an analgesic and antipyretic drug. Analgesics are drugs which relieve pain. Antipyretics are drugs which lower body temperature.

The main constituent of aspirin tablets is 2-ethanoylhydroxybenzoic acid (acetylsalicylic acid, $CH_3COOC_6H_4COOH$, figure 1). The acidic conditions in the stomach do not affect aspirin. However, the alkaline juices in the intestines hydrolyse aspirin to ethanoate (acetate) ions and 2-hydroxybenzoate (salicylate) ions.

$$CH_3COOC_6H_4COOH + 2OH^- \rightarrow$$
$$CH_3COO^- + HOC_6H_4COO^- + H_2O$$

Salicylates lower body temperature rapidly and effectively in feverish patients (antipyretic action), but have little effect if the temperature is normal. They are also mild analgesics, relieving certain types of pain such as headaches and rheumatism.

Although the toxic dose from salicylates is relatively large, their uncontrolled use could be dangerous. Single doses of 5 to 10 g of salicylate have caused death in adults, and 12 g taken over a period of twenty-four hours produces symptoms of poisoning. (A single aspirin tablet containing 0.3 g of acetylsalicylic acid would produce 0.25 g of salicylate when hydrolysed.)

Principle

The object of this experiment is to determine the percentage of 2-ethanoylhydroxybenzoic acid (acetylsalicylic acid) in aspirin tablets. A known amount of standard sodium hydroxide solution is used in excess to hydrolyse a known mass of aspirin tablets.

$$CH_3COOC_6H_4COOH + 2NaOH \rightarrow$$
$$CH_3COONa + HOC_6H_4COONa + H_2O$$

The unused sodium hydroxide which remains is then titrated with standard acid. The amount of alkali required for the hydrolysis can now be calculated and from the above equation, the amount in moles of acetylsalicylic acid which has been hydrolysed can be found.

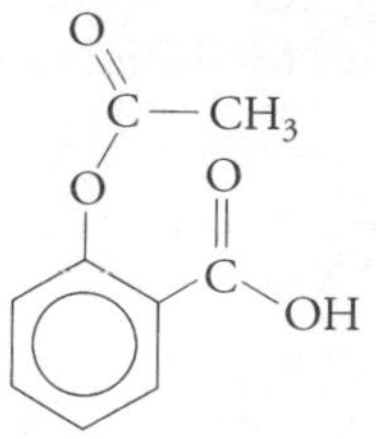

Figure 1
2-Ethanoylhydroxybenzoic acid (acetylsalicylic acid).

Procedure

EYE PROTECTION MUST BE WORN

HIGHLY FLAMMABLE Indicator solution

CORROSIVE Sodium hydroxide solution

> **CARE!**
> *Eye protection must be worn.*

Work in pairs.

Partner No. 1 should standardise the approximately 1.0 mol dm⁻³ NaOH used for the hydrolysis as follows.

Using a safety filler, pipette exactly 25 cm³ of the approximately 1.0 mol dm⁻³ NaOH solution into a 250 cm³ standard flask and make up to the mark. Now titrate 25 cm³ of this solution against 0.10 mol dm⁻³ hydrochloric acid using phenol red (or phenolphthalein) indicator.

Carry out one rough and two accurate titrations.

---

1 Record your results in a table similar to the one below.

Titration number	Rough	Accurate 1	Accurate 2
Final burette reading/cm³ Initial burette reading/cm³			
Volume of 0.1 mol dm⁻³ HCl added/cm³			

2 Calculate the accurate concentration, in mol dm⁻³, of the approximately1.0 mol dm⁻³ NaOH.

Partner No. 2 should hydrolyse the aspirin as follows.

HARMFUL Aspirin

Weigh accurately between 1.3 g and 1.7 g of the aspirin tablets into a clean conical flask. (This will be about 5 tablets.) **Using a safety filler, pipette 25 cm³ of the approximately 1.0 mol dm⁻³ NaOH on to the tablets, followed by about the same volume of distilled water.** Simmer the mixture gently on a tripod and gauze over a bunsen for 10 minutes to hydrolyse the acetylsalicylic acid.

Now, cool the mixture and transfer with washings to a 250 cm³ standard flask and make up to the mark with distilled water.

---

3 Record the mass of aspirin tablets taken.

4 Why is the mixture simmered gently and carefully during hydrolysis? Why is it unwise to boil it vigorously?

5 Why should the washings be transferred carefully to the 250 cm³ standard flask?

Both partners should now estimate the quantity of unused NaOH after the hydrolysis as follows.

Pipette 25 cm³ the hydrolysed solution into a conical flask. Titrate this against 0.10 mol dm⁻³ hydrochloric acid using phenol red (or phenolphthalein) indicator.

6 Record your titration results in a table similar to that in question 1.

7 How many moles of NaOH

a are added to the flask before hydrolysis of the aspirin,
b remain after hydrolysis of the aspirin,
c are used in the hydrolysis of the aspirin?

8 How many moles of acetylsalicylic acid have been hydrolysed?

9 What percentage of the aspirin tablets is acetylsalicylic acid?

10 What might the remainder of the tablets be made of?

11 Look at the packet from which the aspirin tablets came. What mass of acetylsalicylic acid does it say they contain? Compare this with your own results.

Practical 3

Analysing iron tablets

REQUIREMENTS

Each pair of students will need:

Eye protection

Iron tablets (5), sold by chemists as ferrous sulphate tablets

1.0 mol dm^{-3} sulphuric acid (**irritant**) (200 cm^3)

0.01 mol dm^{-3} potassium manganate(VII) (75 cm^3). Dissolve 1.58 g in distilled water and make up to 1 dm^3 (**solid is oxidising and harmful**)

2 conical flasks (250 cm^3)

Standard flask (250 cm^3)

Burette and stand

Pipette (25 cm^3) and safety filler

Filter funnel

Filter paper

Wash bottle and distilled water

Time required $1\frac{1}{4}$ hours

Introduction

Iron is essential to the human body. Its principal role is as a constituent of haemoglobin, the oxygen-carrying agent in the blood. Iron is also present in a number of enzymes and co-enzymes involved in redox processes in the body.

Some groups in the population need substantial amounts of iron in their diet in order to produce extra haemoglobin. Such people include growing children, pregnant and menstruating women, and people who have for various reasons lost considerable amounts of blood. A satisfactory intake of iron can normally be ensured by eating a suitable diet, because certain foods – liver, kidney, egg yolk and spinach for example – are rich in iron. Nevertheless, it is sometimes necessary to supplement the iron taken in the natural diet with 'iron tablets'.

Iron tablets bought at the chemist usually contain iron(II) sulphate (ferrous sulphate) a cheap, soluble form of iron. In this practical you will attempt to find the actual percentage of iron(II) sulphate in the tablets and then compare this result with the quantity stated on the bottle.

Assuming all the iron in the tablets is in the form of Fe^{2+}, it is possible to estimate the iron content by titration against potassium manganate(VII), KMnO$_4$.

The equation for the reaction of Fe^{2+} with MnO$_4^-$ in acid solution is:

$$5Fe^{2+}(aq) + MnO_4^-(aq) + 8H^+(aq) \rightarrow 5Fe^{3+}(aq) + Mn^{2+}(aq) + 4H_2O(l)$$

> **1** How many moles of Fe^{2+} react with 1 mole of MnO$_4^-$?

Procedure

EYE PROTECTION MUST BE WORN   **IRRITANT** Dilute sulphuric acid

> **CARE!**
> *Eye protection must be worn.*

Making a solution of the tablets

Weigh accurately 5 of the iron tablets, then dissolve them in about 100 cm^3 of 1.0 mol dm^{-3} sulphuric acid in a conical flask. This will probably require heating, but do not heat more than necessary to dissolve the tablets.

> **2** Why should the tablets not be heated more than necessary?
>
> **3** Why are the tablets dissolved in sulphuric acid instead of water?

The outer coating of the tablets will probably not dissolve, so the solution will need filtering.

> **4** What do you think the outer coating might be?

Filter the mixture into a beaker, making sure you do not lose any of the solution, then wash out the conical flask with water and pour the washings through the filter. Finally pour distilled water over the residue and collect these washings as well. Pour the filtrate into a 250 cm³ standard flask, washing out the beaker and adding the washings to the standard flask. Make up to the mark with distilled water.

Titration with potassium manganate(VII)

Using a safety filler, pipette 25 cm³ of the iron(II) solution from the beaker into a conical flask. Add about 25 cm³ of 1.0 mol dm⁻³ sulphuric acid and titrate with 0.01 mol dm⁻³ potassium manganate(VII) solution. Repeat until two consistent results are obtained.

> **5** How many moles of MnO_4^- were needed to react with 25 cm³ of your Fe^{2+} solution?
>
> **6** How many moles of Fe^{2+} are there in 25 cm³ of the solution?
>
> **7** How many moles of Fe^{2+} are there in all the tablets?
>
> **8** How many moles of Fe^{2+} are there in one tablet?
>
> **9** What mass of: **a** Fe, **b** $FeSO_4$, **c** $FeSO_4.7H_2O$ is there in one tablet?
>
> **10** What mass of iron(II) sulphate is stated by the makers to be present in each tablet?
>
> **11** Compare your result with the mass stated by the makers, and comment.

Investigation

See
Investigation L1

Practical 4

Titrations involving iodine and thiosulphate. Determining the percentage of copper in brass

REQUIREMENTS

Each student, or pair of students, will need:

Eye protection

Burette and stand

Pipette (25 cm³) and safety filler

Conical titration flask (250 cm³)

Measuring cylinder (25 or 50 cm³)

Small beaker

Beaker (250 cm³)

Standard flask (250 cm³)

2 test tubes

Concentrated nitric acid (**corrosive**)

Hydrogen peroxide solution (6%, or '20 volume') (**irritant**)

Dilute sulphuric acid (1 mol dm⁻³) (**irritant**)

Distilled water

Sodium carbonate solution (1.0 mol dm⁻³)

Dilute ethanoic (acetic) acid (2 mol dm⁻³) (**irritant**)

Approx. 1 mol dm⁻³ KI (30 cm³). Dissolve 166 g of KI in distilled water and make up to 1 dm³

0.1 mol dm⁻³ $Na_2S_2O_3$ (100 cm³). Dissolve 24.8 g of $Na_2S_2O_3.5H_2O$ in distilled water and make up to 1 dm³

Starch solution (6 cm³). Make 2 g of soluble starch and 0.01 g of $HgCl_2$ (**toxic solid**) into a thin paste with water. Add slowly to 1 dm³ of boiling water with stirring. Boil for a few minutes and cool.

Brass (about 3 g) (brass screws are ideal)

Access to balance

Time required $1\frac{1}{4}$ hours

> **CARE!**
> *Eye protection must be worn for both experiment 1 and experiment 2.*

EYE PROTECTION MUST BE WORN

Experiment 1:
Titrations involving iodine and thiosulphate

Iodine/thiosulphate titrations are used to determine the concentration of solutions of oxidising agents.

A known volume of the oxidising agent is first added to an excess of acidified potassium iodide solution. This produces iodine. The iodine is then estimated by titration against standard sodium thiosulphate solution.

A Add a few drops of hydrogen peroxide solution (an oxidising agent) to a mixture of 3 cm³ of KI(aq) and 3 cm³ of dilute H_2SO_4. Keep the final solution for part **B**.

IRRITANT
Dilute sulphuric acid

> 1 Describe and explain what happens.
>
> 2 H_2O_2 acts according to the half equation,
>
> $$H_2O_2 + 2H^+ + 2e^- \longrightarrow 2H_2O$$
>
> Write a half-equation for the oxidation of iodide ions to iodine.

B Add sodium thiosulphate solution to the final mixture from part **A** until no further changes occur.

> 3 Describe and explain what happens.
>
> 4 Thiosulphate ions, $S_2O_3^{2-}$, are oxidised by iodine according to the half-equation:
>
> $$2S_2O_3^{2-} \longrightarrow S_4O_6^{2-} + 2e^-$$
>
> Write an equation for the reduction of iodine by $S_2O_3^{2-}$.
>
> 5 How many moles of $S_2O_3^{2-}$ react with one mole of I_2?

In iodine/thiosulphate titrations, a standard solution of sodium thiosulphate is added from a burette to the iodine solution. In these circumstances, the colour changes from a pale yellow solution of I_2 to a clear solution of I^- ions at the end-point. Generally, however, starch is added to improve the detection of the end-point. Starch forms a deep blue colour with iodine. This dark blue colour disappears at the end-point. The starch should not be added until the iodine has been reduced to a pale yellow colour. Otherwise, iodine becomes strongly adsorbed on to the starch and the titration is less accurate.

Experiment 2:
Determining the percentage of copper in brass

In this experiment, a weighed sample of brass is first reacted with nitric acid. This produces a solution of copper(II) ions. When this solution is treated with aqueous potassium iodide, copper(I) iodide is precipitated as a white solid, and iodine is produced

$$2Cu^{2+}(aq) + 4I^-(aq) \rightarrow 2CuI(s) + I_2(aq)$$

The liberated iodine can then be estimated using standard sodium thiosulphate solution. Knowing the amount of iodine formed, the mass of copper in the original sample of brass can be calculated.

EYE PROTECTION MUST BE WORN

CORROSIVE
Concentrated nitric acid

USE A FUME CUPBOARD

TOXIC
Nitrogen dioxide

> **CARE!**
> *Eye protection must be worn when working with concentrated nitric acid. Any splashes on the skin must be washed off at once.*

> **CARE!**
> *Toxic nitrogen dioxide is evolved. This reaction must be carried out in a fume cupboard.*

Weigh accurately between 2.5 g and 3.0 g of brass. React this brass with the minimum quantity of concentrated nitric acid in a 250 cm³ beaker. About 20 cm³ of concentrated nitric acid should be sufficient.

Transfer the solution, with washings from the beaker, to a 250 cm³ standard flask. Make up the solution to the mark and mix well.

Using a safety filler, pipette 25 cm³ of the brass solution into a conical flask and add sodium carbonate solution until a slight permanent precipitate is obtained. This neutralises excess nitric acid in the solution. Dissolve the precipitate in the minimum volume of dilute ethanoic(acetic) acid and then add 10 cm³ of approximately 1 mol dm⁻³ KI.

IRRITANT
Dilute
ethanoic(acetic) acid

Finally, titrate the liberated iodine against standard 0.1 mol dm⁻³ sodium thiosulphate solution, adding about 2 cm³ of starch indicator when the iodine colour is pale yellow.

Repeat the titration until two consistent results are obtained.

> 6 Describe what happens when:
>
> **a** brass is treated with concentrated HNO_3.
> **b** $Cu^{2+}(aq)$ is treated with KI(aq).
>
> 7 Record your results in a table similar to the one overleaf.

Titration number		Rough	Accurate 1	Accurate 2
Final burette reading/cm³				
Initial burette reading/cm³				
Vol. of 0.1 mol dm⁻³ Na₂S₂O₃ added/cm³				
Average accurate titration =	cm³			

8   Why is it necessary to neutralise the excess nitric acid used to dissolve the brass? (Hint: nitric acid is an oxidising agent.)

9   Write an equation for the neutralisation of excess nitric acid with sodium carbonate solution.

10   How many moles of $S_2O_3^{2-}$ react during titration?

11   How many moles of I_2 react with this amount of $S_2O_3^{2-}$?

12   How many moles of Cu^{2+} ions liberate this amount of I_2?

13   How many moles of Cu^{2+} ions are there in the 250 cm³ of 'brass solution'?

14   How many grams of copper are there in 250 cm³ of 'brass solution'? (Cu = 63.5)

15   What is the percentage by mass of copper in the brass?

Investigation

See
Investigation L6

Studying redox reactions

REQUIREMENTS

Each student, or pair of students, will need:

Eye protection

6 test tubes

Universal indicator paper

Splints

Dilute sulphuric acid (1 mol dm^{-3}) (**irritant**)

Sodium chlorate(I) (hypochlorite) solution (about 1 mol dm^{-3}) (**irritant**)

0.5 mol dm^{-3} aqueous iodine. Dissolve 127g iodine (**irritant**) and 100g KI in distilled water and make up to 1 dm^3

Starch solution (see Practical 4)

Hydrogen peroxide solution (6%, or '20 volume') (**irritant**)

Sulphurous acid (a solution of sulphur dioxide in water) (**harmful, releases a toxic gas**)

Chlorine water (**releases toxic gas**)

Solutions of the following at concentrations of about 1 mol dm^{-3}:

iron(III) chloride

potassium iodide

iron(II) sulphate

potassium bromide or sodium bromide

Time required 1 hour

Introduction

Redox reactions involve electron transfer. When a substance is oxidised it loses electrons, and the substance that received the electrons is reduced. If a substance has a strong tendency to lose electrons it behaves as a **strong reducing agent** because it will tend to reduce other substances by giving them electrons. If a substance has a strong tendency to gain electrons it behaves as a **strong oxidising agent** because of its readiness to gain electrons from other substances and oxidise them.

The intention of this practical is to investigate reactions between pairs of substances which can behave as oxidising and reducing agents, and try to place these substances in order of strength as oxidisers or reducers.

Consider the reaction between chlorine water and a solution containing iodide ions. The mixture turns brown rapidly as iodide ions are oxidised to iodine molecules. At the same time, chlorine molecules are reduced to chloride ions:

$$2I^-(aq) + Cl_2(aq) \rightarrow I_2(aq) + 2Cl^-(aq)$$

Chlorine molecules and chloride ions can be regarded as a **redox pair** and this is summarised in the following half-equation:

$$Cl_2 + 2e^- \rightleftharpoons 2Cl^-$$

When chlorine acts as an oxidiser, it accepts electrons and this half-equation moves from left to right. When chloride ions act as a reducer, they lose electrons and the half-equation moves from right to left. We can think of the I_2/I^- pair acting in the same way:

$$I_2 + 2e^- \rightleftharpoons 2I^-$$

In the reaction between chlorine and iodide, it is impossible for both the half-equations $Cl_2 + 2e^- \rightleftharpoons 2Cl^-$ and $I_2 + 2e^- \rightleftharpoons 2I^-$ to move in the same direction, because there would be nothing to provide the electrons needed by both half-equations. One of the half-equations must move from right to left instead of left to right.

The results of the reaction tells us that it is the iodine/iodide equation that moves from right to left. This is because chlorine molecules have a greater tendency to accept electrons than iodine molecules. In other words chlorine is a stronger oxidiser than iodine. Of course, at the start of the reaction neither iodine nor chloride ions were present, so the reaction could not have proceeded in the other direction in any case. But, if the reaction is carried out with chlorine, chloride ions, iodine and iodide ions all present, the result is still the same – chlorine oxidises iodide to iodine. We can therefore put the two half-equations in order of the tendency to proceed to the right. This shows the order of strength of the oxidising agents.

Increasing oxidising strength $\uparrow$ $\quad$ $\begin{array}{l} Cl_2 + 2e^- \rightleftharpoons 2Cl^- \\[6pt] I_2 + 2e^- \rightleftharpoons 2I^- \end{array}$

In this practical you will be trying to put a number of redox pairs in order of oxidising strength by studying simple test tube reactions. The redox pairs you will be studying are:

A $\quad I_2 + 2e^- \rightleftharpoons 2I^-$
B $\quad SO_4^{2-} + H^+ + e^- \rightleftharpoons H_2SO_3 + H_2O$
C $\quad ClO^- + H_2O + e^- \rightleftharpoons Cl^- + OH^-$
D $\quad Cl_2 + 2e^- \rightleftharpoons 2Cl^-$
E $\quad Br_2 + 2e^- \rightleftharpoons 2Br^-$
F $\quad Fe^{3+} + e^- \rightleftharpoons Fe^{2+}$

ClO^- is called chlorate(I) (hypochlorite) ion, and H_2SO_3 is sulphurous acid.

1 Half-equations **B** and **C** are not balanced. Answer the following questions for each of equations **B** and **C**.

    a Which element is undergoing redox?
    b Work out the oxidation number of this element in both its oxidised and reduced forms.
    c Balance the half-equation.

Procedure

**EYE PROTECTION
MUST BE WORN**

CARE!
Eye protection must be worn for all these experiments.

Experiments 1–6:
Putting the half-equations in order of oxidising strength

Experiment 1

Add 3 cm^3 of a solution of iron(III) ions to a solution of iodide ions. Describe what happens and test to see if iodine has been formed.

The half-equations involved are:

A $\quad I_2 + 2e^- \rightleftharpoons 2I^-$
F $\quad Fe^{3+} + e^- \rightleftharpoons Fe^{2+}$

2 Use these half-equations to write a balanced ionic equation for the reaction that has occurred.

3 In this reaction, which of the half-equations moved from right to left instead of left to right?

4 Place **A** and **F** in order of oxidising strength.

Experiment 2

IRRITANT
Sodium chlorate(I)
solution

Add 3 cm^3 of sodium chlorate(I) solution to a solution containing iron(II) ions. Decide whether or not Fe^{2+} ions have been oxidised. (Note: when chlorate(I) acts as an oxidising agent, hydroxide ions are produced. What effect will this have on iron(II) or iron(III) ions?)

> 5 Place half-equation **C** in its correct position relative to **A** and **F**.
>
> 6 Write a balanced ionic equation for the reaction.

Experiment 3

Add 3 cm^3 of sodium chlorate(I) solution to a solution containing bromide ions. Decide whether or not bromide ions have been oxidised to bromine.

> 7 Can chlorate(I) ions oxidise bromide to bromine?
>
> 8 Place half-equation **E** in its correct position in the list.
>
> 9 Write a balanced ionic equation for the reaction.

Experiment 4

HARMFUL
Sulphurous acid
releases toxic
sulphur dioxide

Add 3 cm^3 of sulphurous acid to a solution containing iodine, I$_2$, and note the result.

> 10 Place half-equation **B** in its correct position in the list.
>
> 11 Write a balanced ionic equation for the reaction.

Experiment 5

TOXIC
Chlorine gas released
from chlorine water

Finally, decide the position of half-equation **D** by adding chlorine water to a solution containing bromide ions.

> 12 Place half-equation **D** in its correct position.
>
> 13 Write a balanced ionic equation for the reaction.
>
> 14 Use your final order of oxidising power to predict whether chlorate(I) ions will oxidise iodide ions to iodine.

Experiment 6

Test your prediction experimentally.

IRRITANT
Hydrogen peroxide
solution

Hydrogen peroxide, H_2O_2 can behave as both an oxidiser and a reducer depending on the conditions. Half-equation **G** shows hydrogen peroxide behaving as an oxidising agent.

G $H_2O_2 + 2H^+ + 2e^- \rightleftharpoons 2H_2O$

Half-equation **H** shows hydrogen peroxide behaving as a reducing agent.

H $O_2 + 2H^+ + 2e^- \rightleftharpoons H_2O_2$

When hydrogen peroxide acts as a reducing agent, half-equation **H** will, of course, occur from right to left.

Experiment 7

Add a little hydrogen peroxide solution to a solution of sodium chlorate(I) and note what happens. Decide whether the hydrogen peroxide is behaving as an oxidiser or as a reducer.

15 Which half-equation **G** or **H**, describes the behaviour of hydrogen peroxide in this experiment?

16 Decide whether this half-equation should be placed above or below half-equation **C**. (It will be impossible to determine the exact position of this half-equation in your list.)

17 Write a balanced ionic equation for the reaction of hydrogen peroxide with chlorate(I) ions.

IRRITANT
Dilute sulphuric acid

Experiment 8

Acidify a little potassium iodide solution with dilute sulphuric acid. Now add a little hydrogen peroxide solution. Describe what happens.

18 Is hydrogen peroxide behaving as an oxidiser or as a reducer in this case?

19 Which half-equation describes the behaviour of hydrogen peroxide in this reaction?

20 Decide whether this half-equation should be placed above or below half-equation **A**.

21 Write a balanced ionic equation for the reaction of hydrogen peroxide with iodide ions in acid solution.

When hydrogen peroxide is left for some time, it slowly decomposes into water and oxygen. This decomposition is speeded up by various catalysts, such as manganese(IV) oxide. The equation for the reaction is:

$$2H_2O_2 \rightarrow 2H_2O + O_2$$

22 Work out the oxidation number of oxygen in H_2O_2, H_2O and O_2.

23 Does the conversion of hydrogen peroxide to **oxygen** involve oxidation or reduction? What substance is acting as the oxidiser or reducer?

24 Does the conversion of hydrogen peroxide to **water** involve oxidation or reduction? What substance is acting as the oxidiser or reducer?

25 Show how the equation for the decomposition of hydrogen peroxide can be derived from half equations **G** and **H**.

26 Explain what is meant by the term **disproportionation**.

Further work

If you have time, devise tests to establish more precisely the positions of **G** and **H** in the list.

Structure, bonding and properties

REQUIREMENTS

Each student, or pair of students, will need:

Eye protection

Polythene rod and fur for charging

Burette

3 beakers (100 cm³)

Rack with 6 test tubes

Pair of carbon electrodes*

100 mA ammeter*

6 V battery or power pack*

Leads and crocodile clips*

Iodine (**harmful**)

Calcium chloride (solid) (**irritant**)

Powdered graphite

Ethanol (**highly flammable**)

Hexane (**highly flammable**)

Distilled water

Silver nitrate solution (about 0.1 mol dm⁻³)

Ethyl ethanoate (ethyl acetate) (**highly flammable**)

Cyclohexane (**highly flammable**)

* One set of these items could be shared by three or four students

Time required 2 hours

HARMFUL
Hexane

HIGHLY FLAMMABLE
Hexane
Ethanol

CARE!
Highly flammable liquids. No flames.

Introduction

Most of the physical and chemical properties of a substance can be related to the type of bonding present in it. In this practical you will study properties such as volatility and conductivity and try to explain these properties in terms of the bonding in the substance involved.

Substances that are ionically bonded contain positive and negative ions. Substances that are covalently bonded contain molecules. If these molecules contain different elements, they may be polar due to the unequal sharing of electrons between the different atoms. The degree of polarity in a molecule, determined by the shape of the molecule and the relative electronegativities of the atoms in it, has a significant effect on the properties of the substance.

Procedure

EYE PROTECTION MUST BE WORN

CARE!
Wear eye protection for all these experiments.

Experiment 1:
The effect of a charged rod on thin streams of liquid

Charge a polythene rod by rubbing it on a piece of fur. Hold the rod about 1 cm from a thin stream of water running from a burette. Note what happens.

1 What sort of particles does water contain?

2 Are these particles polar?

3 Explain the effect of the charged rod on the stream of water.

4 What do you think would happen with a rod of opposite charge? Explain your answer.

Repeat the experiment using hexane, and then ethanol, instead of water.

5 Relate the behaviour of streams of these liquids towards a charged rod to the nature of the particles they contain.

6 Look up the boiling points and relative molecular masses of water, ethanol and hexane. Try to explain the relative magnitudes of their boiling points in terms of polarity.

Experiment 2:
Miscibility of liquids

Test the miscibility of **a** water and ethanol, **b** water and hexane,
c hexane and ethanol.

> 7   Try to explain the results of experiment 2 in terms of the
>   polarities of the molecules in the different liquids.

Experiment 3:
The solubility of iodine in different liquids

CORROSIVE
Iodine

HARMFUL
Iodine

Keep the solutions from this experiment and from experiments **4** and **5**
for use in experiment **7**.

Put a very small crystal of iodine in a test tube. Add 5 cm^3 of distilled
water, put a stopper in the tube and shake. Try to decide roughly how
soluble iodine is in water. Repeat the experiment using ethanol as the
solvent instead of water, and finally using hexane as the solvent.

> 8   What sort of particles does iodine contain?
>
> 9   What forces hold these particles together?
>
> 10 Explain the relative solubility of iodine in the three solvents.
>
> 11 Why do you think iodine is a different colour in different
>   solvents?

Experiment 4:
The solubility of graphite in liquids

Repeat experiment **3**, using powdered graphite instead of iodine.
Answer questions **8** to **10** with reference to graphite instead of iodine.

Experiment 5:
The solubility of calcium chloride in liquids

IRRITANT
Calcium chloride

Repeat experiment **3**, using calcium chloride instead of iodine. As
solutions of calcium chloride are colourless, use the following
procedure to decide how much has dissolved.

After shaking the crystal with the solvent, decant the liquid into a test
tube, leaving the excess crystal behind. Add 2 cm^3 of silver nitrate
solution to the decanted liquid and shake. Judge the relative solubility
of calcium chloride in the three solvents from the amount of silver
chloride precipitated.

Answer questions **8** to **10** with reference to calcium chloride instead of
iodine.

HARMFUL
Iodine

CORROSIVE
Iodine

Experiment 6:
The volatility of iodine, graphite and calcium chloride

> **CARE!**
> *Iodine vapour is corrosive and toxic. Use only a very small crystal of iodine and work in a fume cupboard.*

Heat a crystal of each of the solids in turn in a hard-glass test tube and judge their relative volatilities.

> **12** Try to explain the relative volatility of these three solids in terms of the particles they contain and the forces between them.

Experiment 7:
Conductivity

Collect each of the solutions produced in experiments 3, 4 and 5. Test the conductivity of each solution by the following procedure.

Connect a pair of carbon electrodes in series with a 6 V battery and a 100 mA ammeter. Dip the electrodes in the solution under test and note the meter reading in each case. Test the same depth of solution each time. (If the solid showed no sign of dissolving, do not bother to perform the test in that particular case.) You should also test the conductivity of each of the pure solvents.

Note: keep the electrodes clean and make sure they are not contaminated with liquid from a previous test.

> **13** Try to explain the relative conductivities of the different solutions.

Experiment 8:
The colour of iodine in solution

HIGHLY FLAMMABLE
Ethanol
Hexane
Ethyl ethanoate
Cyclohexane

HARMFUL
Hexane

If you have time, try the following tests. Then see if you can explain the different colours of iodine in different solvents.

A Find the colour of iodine in solution in the following solvents: hexane, ethanol, ethyl ethanoate, cyclohexane.

B Add one drop of ethanol to a solution of iodine in hexane.

C Add one drop of hexane to a solution of iodine in ethanol.

> **CARE!**
> *Flammable liquids. No flames.*

> **14** What is the colour of iodine vapour?
>
> **15** Try to explain the variation of colour of iodine in different solvents.

Investigation
See
Investigation S4

Practical 7

Enthalpy changes of neutralisation

REQUIREMENTS

Each student, or pair of students, will need:

Eye protection

Plastic beaker (the sort used in drink dispensing machines are ideal)

0–100°C thermometer

Measuring cylinder (50 cm³)

The following solutions:

- 2.0 mol dm⁻³ nitric acid (25 cm³). Make 128 cm³ of concentrated acid up to 1 dm³ (**corrosive**)

- 2.0 mol dm⁻³ hydrochloric acid (100 cm³). Make 172 cm³ of concentrated acid up to 1 dm³ (**irritant**)

- 2.0 mol dm⁻³ sulphuric acid (50 cm³). Make 107 cm³ of concentrated acid up to 1 dm³ (**corrosive**)

- 2.0 mol dm⁻³ sodium hydroxide (75 cm³). Dissolve 80 g of pellets or flakes in distilled water and make up to 1 dm³ (**corrosive**)

- 4.0 mol dm⁻³ sodium hydroxide (25 cm³). Dissolve 160 g of pellets or flakes in distilled water and make up to 1 dm³ (**corrosive**)

- 2.0 mol dm⁻³ potassium hydroxide (25 cm³). Dissolve 112 g of pellets in distilled water and make up to 1 dm³ (**corrosive**)

Time required 1 hour

CORROSIVE
Sodium hydroxide solution
Potassium hydroxide solution

EYE PROTECTION MUST BE WORN

IRRITANT
Hydrochloric acid

CARE!
Take care making up the solutions. Concentrated acids and solid alkalis are corrosive. Eye protection is essential.

Introduction

When an acid neutralises an alkali, a salt and water are formed. Aqueous hydrogen ions (H^+(aq)) from the acid react with the hydroxide ions (OH^-(aq)) from the alkali, forming water. For example, when hydrochloric acid and sodium hydroxide react:

$$H^+(aq) + Cl^-(aq) + Na^+(aq) + OH^-(aq) \rightarrow Na^+(aq) + Cl^-(aq) + H_2O(l)$$

hydrochloric acid   sodium hydroxide   sodium chloride

Notice in this equation that the Na^+ and Cl^- ions are unchanged. The only chemical reaction that occurs is between H^+ and OH^- ions:

$$H^+(aq) + OH^-(aq) \rightarrow H_2O(l)$$

The combination of H^+ and OH^- ions releases energy. In this practical, we shall be measuring the enthalpy changes for different neutralisation reactions. Because the number of moles of water formed varies according to the acid and alkali used, it is the convention to measure enthalpies of neutralisation in kilojoules per mole of water formed.

Procedure

CARE!
Wear eye protection for all these experiments.

Experiment 1:
The reaction between hydrochloric acid and sodium hydroxide

Measure 25 cm³ of 2.0 mol dm⁻³ hydrochloric acid into a plastic beaker. Record its temperature. Put 25 cm³ of 2.0 mol dm⁻³ sodium hydroxide solution in a measuring cylinder and take its temperature. Now pour this into the acid, stir and take the final temperature.

1 What was the temperature rise? (If the acid and alkali were not at the same temperature initially, use the average of their initial temperatures as the starting temperature.)

2 How much energy was given to the 50 cm³ of final solution during the reaction? (Assume the specific heat capacity of the plastic cup is negligible, and that the specific heat capacity of the solution is 4.2 J g⁻¹K⁻¹.)

3 How many moles of water were formed in the reaction you have just carried out?

4 Work out the enthalpy change of neutralisation for this reaction in kilojoules per mole of water formed.

Experiment 2:
The reaction between hydrochloric acid and potassium hydroxide

Repeat experiment 1 using 2.0 mol dm^{-3} potassium hydroxide solution instead of the sodium hydroxide.

5 Write an ionic equation like the one in the introduction for the reaction that has occurred.

6 Using the method outlined in questions 1 to 4 above, work out the enthalpy change of neutralisation for this reaction.

Experiment 3:
The reaction between nitric acid and sodium hydroxide

Repeat experiment 1 using 2.0 mol dm^{-3} nitric acid instead of the hydrochloric acid.

CORROSIVE
Nitric acid

7 Write an ionic equation for the reaction which has occurred.

8 Work out the enthalpy change of neutralisation for this reaction.

9 Compare the values you have obtained for the enthalpy changes of neutralisation for the three reactions and explain why the values are similar.

Accepted values for the enthalpy changes of neutralisation of some acids and alkalis are shown in table 1.

Reaction				Enthalpy change of neutralisation /kJ mol^{-1}
HCl(aq) hydrochloric acid	+	NaOH(aq) sodium hydroxide	$\rightarrow$ NaCl(aq) + H$_2$O(l)	−57.9
HNO$_3$(aq) nitric acid	+	NaOH(aq) sodium hydroxide	$\rightarrow$ NaNO$_3$(aq) + H$_2$O(l)	−57.6
HBr(aq) hydrobromic acid	+	NaOH(aq) sodium hydroxide	$\rightarrow$ NaBr(aq) + H$_2$O(l)	−57.6
CH$_3$COOH(aq) ethanoic acid	+	NaOH(aq) sodium hydroxide	$\rightarrow$ CH$_3$COONa(aq) + H$_2$O(l)	−56.1
H$_2$S(aq) hydrogen sulphide	+	NaOH(aq) sodium hydroxide	$\rightarrow$ NaHS(aq) + H$_2$O(l)	−32.2

Table 1

Chemistry in Context Laboratory Manual

10 How do the values for the first two reactions in this table compare with your own experimental results for the same reactions? Account for any errors in your results.

11 Suggest why the enthalpy change of neutralisation for the reaction involving ethanoic acid is slightly lower than the values for the first three reactions, and why the enthalpy change of neutralisation for the reaction involving hydrogen sulphide is substantially lower. (The dissociation constants, K_a, for hydrochloric acid, hydrobromic acid and nitric acid are very large; that for ethanoic acid is 1.7×10^{-5} mol dm^{-3} and that for hydrogen sulphide is 8.9×10^{-8} mol dm^{-3}.)

You should now have some idea of how the relative magnitudes of enthalpy changes of neutralisation can be explained. You can use these ideas in the following experiment.

Experiment 4:
The reaction between sulphuric acid and sodium hydroxide

CORROSIVE
Sulphuric acid

Repeat experiment 1 using 25 cm^3 of 2.0 mol dm^{-3} sulphuric acid and 25 cm^3 of 2.0 mol dm^{-3} sodium hydroxide. Record the temperature rise on mixing as before.

Now repeat the experiment you have just done using 25 cm^3 of 4.0 mol dm^{-3} sodium hydroxide instead of 2.0 mol dm^{-3}.

12 Compare the temperature rises for the two experiments and explain their relative values.

Repeat the experiment using 25 cm^3 of 2.0 mol dm^{-3} hydrochloric acid and 25 cm^3 of 4.0 mol dm^{-3} sodium hydroxide.

13 Compare the temperature rise when 25 cm^3 of 2.0 mol dm^{-3} hydrochloric acid neutralises 25 cm^3 of 2.0 mol dm^{-3} sodium hydroxide with the rise when 4.0 mol dm^{-3} sodium hydroxide is used instead. Explain their relative values. Compare your answer here with your answer to question 12.

Investigation

See
Investigations S1,
S2 and S3

Determining the enthalpy change for the thermal decomposition of potassium hydrogencarbonate

REQUIREMENTS

Each student will need:

Eye protection

Burette and stand

Plastic beaker (approx. 100 cm³) – (the sort used in drink dispensing machines are ideal)

2 clean, dry test tubes

Thermometer (0–50 °C by 0.2 °C is ideal, but one covering 0–110 °C by 1.0 °C can be used)

2 mol dm⁻³ hydrochloric acid (60 cm³) **(irritant)**

Solid anhydrous potassium carbonate (3 g) **(irritant)**

Solid potassium hydrogencarbonate (3.75 g)

Access to a balance

Time required 1 hour

Principle

When potassium hydrogencarbonate, $KHCO_3$, is heated, it decomposes to form potassium carbonate, K_2CO_3. The object of this experiment is to determine the enthalpy change during this reaction. This enthalpy change is difficult to measure directly, so an indirect method is used.

1 Explain the following terms:

  a enthalpy,
  b enthalpy change.

2 Write an equation including state symbols for the thermal decomposition of potassium hydrogencarbonate to potassium carbonate, showing the products in their usual states under standard conditions.

3 What are the standard conditions for thermochemistry?

4 Why is it difficult to determine this enthalpy change directly?

You are provided with 2 mol dm⁻³ hydrochloric acid, solid potassium carbonate and solid potassium hydrogencarbonate. By determining the enthalpy change of reaction between potassium carbonate and hydrochloric acid and that between potassium hydrogencarbonate and hydrochloric acid, it is possible to obtain the enthalpy change for the decomposition of potassium hydrogencarbonate.

Procedure

IRRITANT
Hydrochloric acid
Anhydrous potassium carbonate

EYE PROTECTION MUST BE WORN

> **CARE!**
> *Eye protection must be worn for both experiment 1 and experiment 2.*

Experiment 1:
The reaction of potassium carbonate with hydrochloric acid

Using a burette, measure 30 cm³ of approximately 2 mol dm⁻³ hydrochloric acid into a plastic beaker. Take the temperature of the acid and record this in table 1.

Mass of test tube + potassium carbonate	g
Mass of empty test tube	g
Mass of potassium carbonate used	g
Temperature of acid initially	°C
Temperature of solution after mixing	°C
Temperature change during reaction	°C

Table 1

Accurately weigh a test tube empty and then again when it contains between 2.5 g and 3.0 g of anhydrous potassium carbonate (K_2CO_3). Record the masses in a table similar to table 1.

Now add the weighed portion of K_2CO_3 to the acid and stir the mixture carefully with the thermometer until all the solid has reacted. Rapid effervescence will occur. Be careful not to spill any of the reaction mixture. Record the maximum temperature of the solution after mixing.

> 5 Write an equation, including state symbols, for the reaction between potassium carbonate and hydrochloric acid.
>
> 6 From your results in table 1, calculate the energy released or absorbed during the reaction between the potassium carbonate and the acid.
> (Assume that the specific heat capacities of all the solutions are the same as that of water (i.e. $4.2 \text{ J g}^{-1}\text{K}^{-1}$), and that the solutions have a density of 1.0 g cm^{-3}. Assume that the specific heat capacity of the plastic beaker is negligible.)
>
> 7 Calculate the enthalpy change for one mole of potassium carbonate.
>
> 8 Why is the exact concentration of the acid unimportant?

Experiment 2:
The reaction of potassium hydrogencarbonate with hydrochloric acid

EYE PROTECTION
MUST BE WORN

Repeat experiment 1 using an accurately weighed sample of potassium hydrogencarbonate between 3.25 g and 3.75 g in place of the potassium carbonate. Record all masses and temperatures in a table similar to table 2.

Mass of test tube + potassium hydrogencarbonate	g
Mass of empty test tube	g
Mass of potassium hydrogencarbonate used	g
Temperature of acid initially	°C
Temperature of solution after mixing	°C
Temperature change during reaction	°C

Table 2

9   Write an equation, including state symbols, for the reaction between potassium hydrogencarbonate and hydrochloric acid.

10 From your results in table 2, calculate the energy released or absorbed during the reaction between the potassium hydrogencarbonate and the acid. (You should make the same assumptions as in question 6.)

11 Calculate the enthalpy change for one mole of potassium hydrogencarbonate.

12 State three major sources of error in your experiments.

13 Draw an enthalpy diagram (cycle) linking the decomposition of $KHCO_3(s)$ to $K_2CO_3(s)$, the reaction of $K_2CO_3(s)$ with $HCl(aq)$ and the reaction of $KHCO_3(s)$ with $HCl(aq)$.

14 What is the enthalpy change for the decomposition of potassium hydrogencarbonate?

15 What law have you used in answering question 14 and on what thermodynamic principle does this law depend?

Practical 9

Enthalpy changes of solution

REQUIREMENTS

Each student, or pair of students, will need:

Eye protection

Sodium chloride

Ammonium nitrate (**oxidising**)

Sodium hydroxide (flakes or pellets) (**corrosive**)

Sodium thiosulphate-5-water, $Na_2S_2O_3.5H_2O$

Measuring cylinder (100 cm³)

Thermometer (0–50 °C)

Plastic beaker (the sort used in drink dispensing machines are ideal)

Pestle and mortar

Weighing bottle

Access to a balance

Time required   1 hour

WEAR PROTECTIVE GLOVES

EYE PROTECTION MUST BE WORN

OXIDISING
Ammonium nitrate

CORROSIVE
Sodium hydroxide

Introduction

When an ionic solid dissolves in water to form an aqueous solution, a temperature change is usually observed. In the first part of this practical we shall look in a simple, qualitative way at the magnitude of the temperature changes involved. In the second part, we shall determine an accurate value of the enthalpy change of solution of one ionic solid.

Procedure

Experiment 1:
Temperature changes when different ionic solids dissolve in water

Carry out the following procedure for each of the three solutes: sodium chloride, sodium hydroxide and ammonium nitrate.

> **CARE!**
> *Sodium hydroxide is very corrosive: avoid all contact with the skin and eyes. Eye protection and protective gloves must be worn. If any sodium hydroxide comes into contact with the skin, wash it immediately with plenty of cold water.*

Weigh out 0.1 mol of the solid. In the case of sodium hydroxide the pellets or flakes should be weighed in a sealed weighing bottle.

Measure 100 cm³ of distilled water into a plastic beaker and take its temperature. Quickly dissolve the 0.1 mol of solid in the water, stirring briskly with the thermometer, and record the final temperature.

Make a table for your results, showing the temperature change for each solute.

> 1   Why, apart from the danger of skin contact, is it important to weigh the sodium hydroxide in a sealed bottle?
>
> 2   Which solute, or solutes, gave out energy as they dissolved? Which absorbed energy?

When an ionic solid dissolves in water, two processes occur. First, the ions in the solid lattice must be separated from one another. As the ions carry opposite charges and attract one another, this process of bond-breaking requires the *input* of energy. The second process involves the interaction of the ions of the solute with polar water molecules – positive ions attract the negative ends of H_2O dipoles, and negative ions attract the positive ends. This process of bond-making *gives out* energy. The sign and magnitude of the overall energy change depends on the relative sizes of the energy changes occurring in these two processes.

(See *Chemistry in Context*, Fifth Edition, Section 12.14, for a more detailed consideration of the processes that occur when an ionic solid dissolves.)

3 Explain the temperature changes that occurred when each of the three solutes dissolved in terms of the two energy changes referred to above.

4 If you had used excess solute in your experiment, a saturated solution would have been formed, with undissolved solute in equilibrium with its aqueous solution. For example:

$$NH_4^+NO_3^-(s) + aq \rightleftharpoons NH_4^+(aq) + NO_3^-(aq)$$

By applying Le Chatelier's principle to this equilibrium, decide whether the solubility of ammonium nitrate will increase or decrease when the temperature is raised. How will the solubility of sodium chloride change when the temperature is raised?

Experiment 2:

Measuring the enthalpy change of solution of sodium thiosulphate

The enthalpy change of solution, ΔH_{soln}, of a solute is the enthalpy change that occurs when one mole of the solute dissolves to form an infinitely dilute solution. In this part of the practical you are asked to plan and carry out a simple experiment to obtain as accurate a value as possible for ΔH_{soln} for hydrated sodium thiosulphate, $Na_2S_2O_3.5H_2O$.

In principle this can be done by measuring the temperature change of the water in which the sodium thiosulphate dissolves. But, bear the following points in mind when planning your experiment.

A Heat losses must be minimised. In particular, you will need good insulation and the sodium thiosulphate should be dissolved as quickly as possible. Try to think of other ways of reducing heat losses.

B It will not be possible to make an infinitely dilute solution. Your solution will need to be concentrated enough to produce an accurately measurable temperature rise. Think carefully about the best concentration to use.

C You can assume that the specific heat capacity of sodium thiosulphate solution is the same as that of water, i.e. $4.2 \, J \, g^{-1} K^{-1}$.

D You will need to bear in mind the apparatus available to you.

5 Write a brief description of your experiment and tabulate your results.

6 Work out the value for the enthalpy change of solution of sodium thiosulphate as follows.

a Use the temperature change of the solution to calculate the enthalpy change that occurred in the solution.

b Knowing the amount of sodium thiosulphate used, calculate the enthalpy change that would have occurred if one mole of sodium thiosulphate had been used.

7 What are the major sources of error in your experiment?

8 How could you reduce these errors with more sophisticated apparatus?

9 How would you expect the value of ΔH_{soln} to change if you used *anhydrous* sodium thiosulphate instead of $Na_2S_2O_3.5H_2O$?

10 Strictly speaking, ΔH_{soln} applies to the formation of *infinitely dilute* solutions. What simple experiment could you do with the solution you prepared to decide whether a significant error was introduced by not making it infinitely dilute?

Investigation

See
Investigation S5

Practical 10

Acids, bases and indicators

REQUIREMENTS

Each student, or pair of students, will need:

Eye protection

Rack and 6 test tubes

Dilute hydrochloric acid

Concentrated hydrochloric acid (**corrosive**)

Dilute ethanoic (acetic) acid (**irritant**)

Dilute sodium hydroxide (**corrosive**)

Ammonium chloride solution
(1.0 mol dm^{-3})

Sodium chloride

Sodium ethanoate

Phenol (**toxic** and **corrosive**)

Sodium benzoate

Ethanol (**highly flammable**)

Magnesium powder (**highly flammable**)

Distilled water

Bromophenol blue indicator (if this is not available, methyl orange is equally suitable)

Time required $1\frac{1}{4}$ hours

Introduction

If we define acids as proton donors and bases as proton acceptors, it is clear that every acid must have a corresponding base. This is formed when the acid loses a proton:

$$HA \rightleftharpoons H^+ + A^-$$
acid   base

A^- is said to be the **conjugate base** of the acid HA, and vice versa.

Acids differ widely in their tendency to lose a proton. Acids which donate protons readily are said to be **strong acids**. Strong acids have weak conjugate bases, because the conjugate base will have little tendency to accept the proton back. Weak acids, on the other hand, have strong conjugate bases. For example, hydrochloric acid, HCl, is a strong acid whereas ethanoic acid, CH_3COOH, is weak. From this, it follows that the chloride ion, Cl^-, is a weak base whereas the ethanoate ion, CH_3COO^-, is a stronger base. We can therefore arrange these two acid–base pairs in order of strength as acids and bases.

$$
\begin{array}{ccc}
 & \textbf{Acid} & \textbf{Base} \\
\text{increasing} & HCl \rightleftharpoons H^+ + Cl^- & \text{increasing} \\
\text{acid} & & \text{base} \\
\text{strength} & CH_3COOH \rightleftharpoons H^+ + CH_3COO^- & \text{strength}
\end{array}
$$

This idea has been extended in table 1 to show a number of well-known acids and their conjugate bases in order of strength. Table 1 includes several of the acids you will meet in this practical. Note that ethanol and water appear as acids in table 1, even though both are so weak that they are not normally regarded as acids.

Name of acid	Acid		Base	Name of base
chloric(VII) acid	$HClO_4$	$\rightleftharpoons$	$H^+ + ClO_4^-$	chlorate(VII) ion
hydrochloric acid	HCl	$\rightleftharpoons$	$H^+ + Cl^-$	chloride ion
oxonium ion	H_3O^+	$\rightleftharpoons$	$H^+ + H_2O$	water
methanoic acid	HCOOH	$\rightleftharpoons$	$H^+ + HCOO^-$	methanoate ion
ethanoic acid	CH_3COOH	$\rightleftharpoons$	$H^+ + CH_3COO^-$	ethanoate ion
ammonium ion	NH_4^+	$\rightleftharpoons$	$H^+ + NH_3$	ammonia
phenol	C_6H_5OH	$\rightleftharpoons$	$H^+ + C_6H_5O^-$	phenoxide ion
water	H_2O	$\rightleftharpoons$	$H^+ + {}^-OH$	hydroxide ion
ethanol	CH_3CH_2OH	$\rightleftharpoons$	$H^+ + CH_3CH_2O^-$	ethoxide ion

Table 1
Conjugate acid–base pairs arranged in order of decreasing acid strength

Procedure

**EYE PROTECTION
MUST BE WORN**

CARE!
Eye protection must be worn in all these experiments.

Experiment 1:
Proton-transfer reactions between acids and bases

IRRITANT
Dilute ethanoic acid
Dilute hydrochloric
acid

CARE!
When smelling substances, do so very cautiously. Fill your lungs with air, hold the tube at a distance and waft the gas towards your nose.

1 Do: **a** hydrochloric acid, **b** ethanoic acid, **c** ethanoate ions have characteristic smells?

A Add a little dilute hydrochloric acid to a little solid sodium ethanoate, and warm. Smell the reaction mixture cautiously.

2 Has a proton-transfer reaction occurred? If so, what substance has behaved as an acid, and what has behaved as a base?

B Add a little dilute ethanoic acid to a little solid sodium chloride and warm.

3 Is there any evidence that a proton-transfer reaction has occurred?

C Your observations in this experiment illustrate a simple rule: if an acid, HA_1, is added to the conjugate base, A_2^-, of a weaker acid, HA_2, a proton-transfer reaction occurs, forming A_1^- and HA_2.

$$HA_1 + A_2^- \rightleftharpoons HA_2 + A_1^-$$
stronger   weaker acid
acid

This is because HA_1 has a greater tendency to donate protons than HA_2. This rule can be illustrated further using phenol.

CARE!
Phenol is corrosive and toxic. Eye protection is essential. Avoid all contact with the skin. Wear protective gloves.

**WEAR PROTECTIVE
GLOVES**

CORROSIVE
Phenol

TOXIC
Phenol

Put a few crystals of phenol in a test tube. Add an equal volume of water, cork the tube and shake.

4 Does phenol dissolve in water?

CORROSIVE
Sodium hydroxide
solution

CORROSIVE
Concentrated
hydrochloric acid

D Now add excess of a solution containing hydroxide ions (dilute sodium hydroxide).

5 What happens?

6 A proton-transfer reaction has occurred. What substance has acted as an acid, and what has acted as a base?

E Now add a few drops of concentrated hydrochloric acid.

7 What happens?

8 Another proton-transfer reaction has occurred. What substance has acted as an acid, and what has acted as a base this time?

9 Explain the reactions that have occurred in terms of the relative positions of hydrochloric acid, phenol and water in table 1, page 28.

Experiment 2:
Finding the position of benzoic acid in the table

Benzoic acid, C_6H_5COOH, is a white solid which is nearly insoluble in water. Benzoate ions, however, are soluble.

Make a solution of sodium benzoate by dissolving 1.0 g in 10 cm^3 of water. Divide the solution between three test tubes. To the first tube add 2 cm^3 of dilute hydrochloric acid, to the second 2 cm^3 of dilute ethanoic acid, and to the third 2 cm^3 of a solution containing ammonium ions (ammonium chloride solution). Record your results and write equations where appropriate.

10 Where should benzoic acid be positioned in the table?

Experiment 3:
Acid strength and hydrogen ion concentration

In aqueous solution, acids donate protons to water molecules, forming the oxonium ion, H_3O^+.

$$HA(aq) + H_2O(l) \rightleftharpoons H_3O^+(aq) + A^-(aq)$$

Oxonium ions are often written simply as $H^+(aq)$.

The stronger the acid HA, the further this equilibrium will lie to the right, and the higher the concentration of $H^+(aq)$.

HIGHLY FLAMMABLE
Ethanol

HIGHLY FLAMMABLE
Magnesium powder

Prepare four test tubes as follows:
Tube 1: 4 cm^3 of dilute ethanoic acid
Tube 2: 4 cm^3 of ammonium chloride solution
Tube 3: 4 cm^3 of water
Tube 4: 4 cm^3 of ethanol

To each of these tubes add **half a spatula load** of magnesium powder. Compare the reactions in the different tubes.

11 Write a general ionic equation for the reactions that occur.

12 Relate the vigour of each reaction to the acid strength of the liquid in the tube.

Experiment 4:
Acid–base indicators

Indicators are substances that change colour according to the pH of the solution they are in. Indicators are themselves weak acids or bases which differ in colour from their conjugates.

For example, phenolphthalein, an indicator which is colourless in acid but pink in alkali, is a weak acid which we might represent as HPh. Un-ionised acid, HPh, is colourless, but its conjugate base, Ph⁻, is pink.

$$HPh(aq) \rightleftharpoons H^+(aq) + Ph^-(aq)$$
colourless   pink

When acid is added, the equilibrium moves to the left and the colourless form is in large excess. When alkali is added, $H^+(aq)$ is removed, the equilibrium moves to the right and the pink form predominates. Hence phenolphthalein is colourless in acid but pink in alkali.

Put 2 cm³ of dilute hydrochloric acid in a test tube and add 2 drops of the indicator bromophenol blue, which can be represented as HB.

13 In what form is the indicator present in the tube? What colour is the form?

Add excess sodium hydroxide solution.

14 In what form is the indicator now present? What is the colour of this form?

Prepare five test tubes as follows:
Tube 1: 4 cm³ of dilute hydrochloric acid
Tube 2: 4 cm³ of dilute ethanoic acid
Tube 3: 4 cm³ of ammonium chloride solution
Tube 4: 2 or 3 crystals of phenol (**CARE**) dissolved in 4 cm³ of water
Tube 5: 4 cm³ of water
Add 2 drops of bromophenol blue indicator to each tube and record the colour.

CORROSIVE
Phenol

Investigation
See
Investigation L2

15 Where would you place HB in the table of acids? Why is it not possible to position it exactly?

Practical 11

Electrochemical cells

REQUIREMENTS

Each student, or pair of students, will need:

Eye protection

Test tube

Zinc powder

3 beakers (100 cm³)

2 wire leads fitted with crocodile clips

Access to a high resistance voltmeter. It is best to have at least one meter between three or four pairs.

Strips of filter paper long enough to connect two 100 cm³ beakers

Saturated potassium nitrate solution

Strip of zinc foil about 6 cm × 1 cm

Strip of copper foil about 6 cm × 1 cm

Iron nail

Emery paper

1.0 mol dm⁻³ copper sulphate solution (**harmful**) (50 cm³). Dissolve 250 g of hydrated copper(II) sulphate in distilled water and make up to 1 dm³

0.1 mol dm⁻³ copper sulphate solution (50 cm³)*

0.01 mol dm⁻³ copper sulphate solution (50 cm³)*

0.001 mol dm⁻³ copper sulphate solution (50 cm³)*

1.0 mol dm⁻³ zinc sulphate solution (50 cm³). Dissolve 288 g of hydrated zinc sulphate in distilled water and make up to 1 dm³

1.0 mol dm⁻³ iron(II) sulphate solution (acidified). Dissolve 278 g of hydrated iron(II) sulphate (**harmful**) in 200 cm³ of 1.0 mol dm⁻³ sulphuric acid (**irritant**) and make up to 1 dm³ with distilled water

* Made by diluting the 1.0 mol dm⁻³ solution as appropriate

Time required   1–2 hours

Introduction

Many chemical reactions give out energy. This energy is usually transferred by heating, and when the energy is used, for example to drive an engine, the chemical is called a **fuel**. Occasionally a chemical reaction can be arranged so that the energy is transferred electrically. Such an arrangement is called an **electrochemical cell**.

Procedure

CARE!
Eye protection must be worn in all these experiments.

EYE PROTECTION MUST BE WORN

Introductory experiment

Add a little zinc powder to a few cubic centimetres of 1.0 mol dm⁻³ copper sulphate solution in a test tube. Note everything that happens.

In this reaction, copper(II) ions are being reduced by zinc:

$$Zn(s) + Cu^{2+}(aq) \rightarrow Zn^{2+}(aq) + Cu(s)$$

Electrons are transferred from zinc atoms to copper ions. If the zinc atoms are kept apart from the copper ions, the electrons transferred from Zn to Cu^{2+} can be made to flow down a wire. In this way, the energy transferred by heating in the simple test-tube reaction above can be made available as electricity.

Experiment 1: Constructing a zinc/copper cell

One way of doing this is shown in figure 1 (opposite). A strip of zinc foil is placed in contact with zinc ions, and a strip of copper foil in contact with copper ions. These two **half-cells** are then connected by a wire joining the metal electrodes and a salt bridge connecting the ionic solutions. The following reactions occur:

In the left-hand beaker $Zn(s) \rightarrow Zn^{2+}(aq) + 2e^-$
In the right-hand beaker $Cu^{2+}(aq) + 2e^- \rightarrow Cu(s)$

The electrons flow down the wire from the left-hand to the right-hand beaker, giving an electric current. A potential difference is set up between the two half-cells. This potential difference is at a maximum when no current is flowing, and it is then called the **e.m.f.** of the cell, or E_{cell}. The value of E_{cell} depends on a number of factors, but when the concentrations of zinc and copper ions are both 1.0 mol dm⁻³, E_{cell} is said to have its **standard** value, indicated by $E_{cell}^{\ominus}$. $E_{cell}^{\ominus}$ is usually measured at a temperature of 298 K.

Set up a zinc/copper cell (often called a Daniell cell) as shown in figure 1. Clean the zinc and copper foils with emery before use. Use 1.0 mol dm^{-3} zinc sulphate and 1.0 mol dm^{-3} copper sulphate for the electrolytes, and a strip of filter paper soaked in saturated potassium nitrate solution for the salt bridge.

Measure the e.m.f. of the cell using a high-resistance voltmeter. You should be able to predict the polarity of the electrodes before connecting the meter.

1 What is $E^{\ominus}_{\text{cell}}$ for the zinc/copper cell?

2 Bearing in mind the relative tendencies of zinc, iron and copper to lose electrons, would you expect a zinc/iron cell to have a greater or a smaller $E^{\ominus}_{\text{cell}}$ than a zinc/copper cell?

Experiment 2:
Constructing a zinc/iron cell

HARMFUL
Acidified iron(II) sulphate solution

Set up a zinc/iron cell using a similar arrangement to the previous one, with a Fe/Fe^{2+} half-cell instead of the copper one. (Keep the copper half-cell for a later experiment.) Use a clean iron nail for the iron electrode and an acidified 1.0 mol dm^{-3} iron(II) sulphate solution as the electrolyte. Use a fresh salt bridge. You should be able to predict the polarity of the cell before measuring its e.m.f.

3 Write an equation for the reaction occurring in this cell.

4 What is $E^{\ominus}_{\text{cell}}$ for the zinc/iron cell?

5 Assuming that each half-cell in a cell makes a fixed, independent contribution to $E^{\ominus}_{\text{cell}}$, use your answers to questions 1 and 4 to predict $E^{\ominus}_{\text{cell}}$ for an iron/copper cell.

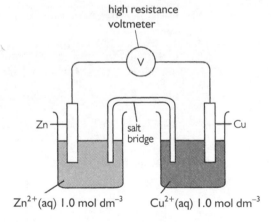

high resistance
voltmeter

V

Zn ———   ——— Cu

salt
bridge

Zn^{2+}(aq) 1.0 mol dm^{-3} Cu^{2+}(aq) 1.0 mol dm^{-3}

Figure 1
A simple cell.

Experiment 3:
Constructing an iron/copper cell

Set up an iron/copper cell using the Fe/Fe^{2+} and Cu/Cu^{2+} half-cells you used in the previous two experiments. Use a fresh salt bridge. Measure $E^{\ominus}_{\text{cell}}$.

6 How does your measured value for $E_{cell}^{\ominus}$ compare with your predicted value?

Experiment 4:
Effect of concentration on E_{cell}

When current is drawn from a Daniell cell, the reactions occurring at each electrode are:

$$Zn(s) \rightarrow Zn^{2+}(aq) + 2e^- \quad \text{and} \quad Cu^{2+}(aq) + 2e^- \rightarrow Cu(s)$$

However, when the e.m.f. of the cell is being measured, no current is being drawn and each electrode is at equilibrium:

$$Zn(s) \rightleftharpoons Zn^{2+}(aq) + 2e^- \quad \text{and} \quad Cu^{2+}(aq) + 2e^- \rightleftharpoons Cu(s)$$

7 Use Le Chatelier's principle to predict the changes that occur if the ion concentration in each equilibrium is reduced.

8 What will be the effect of decreasing the concentration of copper ions on the tendency of the copper electrode to accept electrons from the zinc?

9 What will be the effect on E_{cell} of decreasing the concentration of copper ions?

Test your prediction in question **9** as follows. Set up a Daniell cell as in experiment **1**, and measure E_{cell} with the following concentrations of $Cu^{2+}(aq)$: 0.1 mol dm^{-3}, 0.01 mol dm^{-3}, 0.001 mol dm^{-3}. Use a fresh salt bridge each time. At the lower concentrations, it is very important to pay careful attention to cleanliness in the copper half-cells, as small quantities of impurities will give rise to large errors.

10 Does E_{cell} increase or decrease when $Cu^{2+}(aq)$ concentration decreases?

11 Is the relation between E_{cell} and $Cu^{2+}(aq)$ concentration a linear one? If not, what form does it take?

12 How would E_{cell} change when $Zn^{2+}(aq)$ concentration decreases?

13 The cell shown in figure 2 is an example of a **concentration cell**. Use your experimental results to predict its e.m.f. Check your answer experimentally if you have time.

Investigation

See
Investigation S6

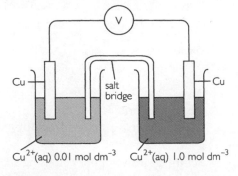

Figure 2
A concentration cell.

Practical 12

Complex formation and competition for cations

REQUIREMENTS

Each student, or pair of students, will need:

Eye protection

6 test tubes

2 teat pipettes

Access to approximately 0.1 mol dm^{-3} solutions of the following:

Iron(III) chloride (**irritant solid**). Dissolve 16.2 g of FeCl$_3$ in distilled water and make up to 1 dm^3.

Potassium thiocyanate (**harmful solid**). Dissolve 9.7 g of KSCN in distilled water and make up to 1 dm^3.

Sodium 2-hydroxybenzoate (salicylate). Dissolve 16.0 g of HOC$_6$H$_4$COONa in distilled water and make up to 1 dm^3.

Edta (disodium salt). Dissolve 33.6 g of [CH$_2$N(CH$_2$COOH).CH$_2$COONa]$_2$ in distilled water and make up to 1 dm^3.

Ammonium ethanedioate (oxalate) (**harmful solid**). Dissolve 14.2 g of (COONH$_4$)$_2$.H$_2$O in distilled water and make up to 1 dm^3.

Silver nitrate (**corrosive solid**)

Sodium chloride

Ammonia (**corrosive when concentrated, releases harmful gas**)

Potassium bromide

Potassium iodide

Sodium thiosulphate

Time required 1 hour

Introduction

In aqueous solution, H$^+$ ions are attached to polar water molecules by co-ordinate bonds forming H$_3$O$^+$ ions (figure 1). In the same way, other cations also exist in aqueous solution as hydrated ions with formulae of the type [M(H$_2$O)$_n$]$^{x+}$.

Figure 1
Co-ordinate bonding in an H$_3$O$^+$ ion.

H$^+$ ions are very small and it is assumed that each one associates with only one water molecule. The larger size of other cations does, however, allow them to associate with two, four or even six water molecules. For example, Ag$^+$ ions exist in aqueous solution as [Ag(H$_2$O)$_2$]$^+$, Cu^{2+} ions exist as [Cu(H$_2$O)$_4$]$^{2+}$ and Fe^{3+} ions exist as [Fe(H$_2$O)$_6$]$^{3+}$.

Other polar molecules, besides water, can also co-ordinate with metal cations. Thus, in aqueous ammonia Cu^{2+} exists mainly as [Cu(NH$_3$)$_4$]$^{2+}$ and Ag$^+$ exists as [Ag(NH$_3$)$_2$]$^+$. Anions, such as Cl$^-$, OH$^-$ and S$_2$O$_3^{2-}$, can also associate with cations in the same way as polar molecules like H$_2$O and NH$_3$. Thus, Ag$^+$ exists as [Ag(S$_2$O$_3$)$_2$]$^{3-}$ in sodium thiosulphate solution and Cu^{2+} ions form [CuCl$_4$]$^{2-}$ in concentrated hydrochloric acid.

Ions such as [Ag(S$_2$O$_3$)$_2$]$^{3-}$ and [Ag(NH$_3$)$_2$]$^+$, in which a metal ion is associated with anions or neutral molecules, are known as **complex ions**. The anions and molecules co-ordinated to the central cation are called **ligands**. Each ligand contains at least one atom bearing a lone pair of electrons which can be donated to the central cation forming a co-ordinate (dative) bond.

Most ligands form only one co-ordinate bond with a cation. These ligands, which include H$_2$O, NH$_3$ and Cl$^-$, are said to be **unidentate** because they have only 'one tooth' with which to attach themselves to the central cation in a complex. (The word 'dens' in Latin means tooth.) In some cases, ligands form two or more co-ordinate bonds to a central metal ion and these ligands are said to be **polydentate**, meaning 'many teeth' (figure 2, overleaf).

Some ligands such as edta (ethylenediaminetetraacetate) in [Ag(edta)]$^{3-}$ can form as many as six co-ordinate bonds with the central ion. The complex ions formed between polydentate ligands and cations are known as **chelates** or **chelated complexes**. The Greek word 'chelos', means 'claw' and the polydentate ligands form a claw-like grip on the central metal ion.

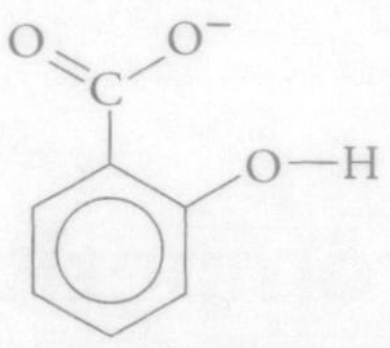

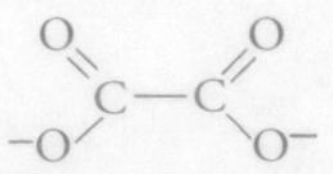

2-hydroxybenzoate ion
(salicylate ion)

ethanedioate ion
(oxalate ion)

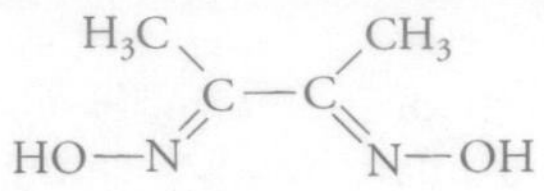

butanedione dioxime
(dimethylglyoxime)

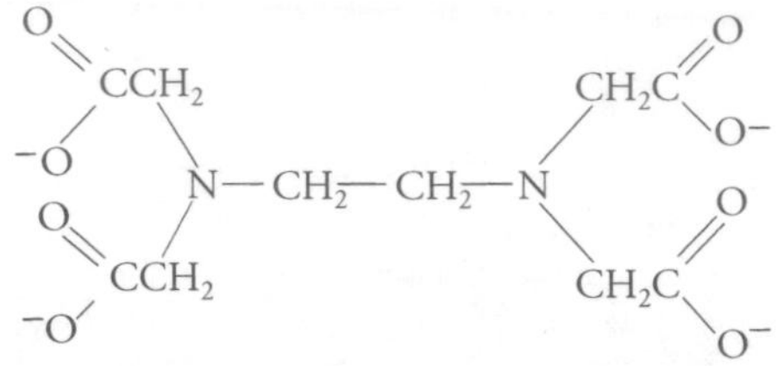

edta
(ethylenediaminetetraacetate ion)

Figure 2
Some polydentate ligands.

The intention of this practical is to study the formation of complexes and to determine the relative strength with which different ligands form complex ions.

Procedure

EYE PROTECTION MUST BE WORN

> **CARE!**
> *Eye protection must be worn for all these experiments.*

Experiment 1:
Complexes in which Fe^{3+} is the central ion

A Put 10 drops of iron(III) chloride solution in a test tube.

> **1** The complex ion in this solution is $[Fe(H_2O)_6]^{3+}$. What is its colour and what ligand does it contain?

B Add potassium thiocyanate solution, KSCN(aq), drop by drop until no further change occurs. (Keep half of the resulting solution for part **E**. Use the other half for part **C**.)

> **2** What is the colour of the solution now? What ligand is present in the complex ion?

C If the solution from **B** is too deeply coloured, dilute it until the true colour of the complex is evident. Now, add sodium 2-hydroxybenzoate (salicylate) solution drop by drop until there is no further change in colour. Keep the solution for part **D**. (The formula of 2-hydroxybenzoate is shown in figure 2.)

3 What is the colour of the solution now? What ligand is now present in the complex ion?

4 Which ligand, NCS^- or $HOC_6H_4COO^-$, competes more strongly for Fe^{3+} ions during complexing?

D Take 10 drops of the solution from **C** and add a solution of edta drop by drop until there is no further colour change.

5 What colour is the edta–Fe(III) complex?

6 Write the ligands NCS^-, $HOC_6H_4COO^-$, edta and water in order of increasing strength of co-ordination with Fe^{3+} ions.

7 Predict what would happen if edta solution were added to the solution obtained in **B**.

E Add edta solution drop by drop to the solution retained in part **B** until there is no further colour change.

8 Was your prediction in question 7 correct?

Experiment 2:
Investigating the relative strength of ethanedioate, $C_2O_4^{2-}$, as a ligand with Fe^{3+}

Add ammonium ethanedioate (oxalate) solution drop by drop to 10 drops of iron(III) chloride solution until there is no further colour change.

9 What is the colour of the solution? What ligand is present in the complex ion?

10 How does ethanedioate compare with water as a ligand?

Devise test tube experiments to find the strength of the ethanedioate ion ($C_2O_4^{2-}$) as a ligand relative to NCS^-, $HOC_6H_4COO^-$ and edta. **After checking with your teacher**, carry out the experiments.

11 Describe the experiments you performed and give the results.

12 Write the five ligands in order of increasing strength.

13 What structural features do the strongest ligands have in common?

Experiment 3:
Complexes in which Ag^+ is the central ion

Some ligands react with cations in aqueous solution to form precipitates of insoluble solids. Ag^+, for example, reacts with Cl^- to form insoluble AgCl. These precipitates can be regarded as neutral complexes. Being uncharged, they are less readily hydrated by polar water molecules than charged complexes. So, they are less likely to dissolve in water.

Put 10 drops of silver nitrate solution into each of six test tubes. To the first tube add 10 drops of sodium chloride solution. To the second tube add 10 drops of ammonia solution; to the third 10 drops of potassium bromide; to the fourth sodium thiosulphate; to the fifth potassium iodide and to the sixth edta solution.

> **14** Make a table showing the ligand added to each tube and the formula, name, state and colour of each complex ion or precipitate.

The relative strengths of the ligands used in the last experiment are:

$$\text{edta} > I^- > S_2O_3^{2-} > Br^- > NH_3 > Cl^- > H_2O$$

You are about to perform an experiment in which first a solution of sodium chloride, then one of ammonia, then one of potassium bromide, then sodium thiosulphate, then potassium iodide and finally edta are added in turn to a solution of Ag^+ ions.

> **15** Use the relative strengths of the ligands to predict what will happen.

Add sodium chloride solution drop by drop to 10 drops of silver nitrate solution until no further change occurs. To the resulting solution add ammonia solution dropwise until no further change occurs. Now add potassium bromide solution dropwise until no further change occurs. Carry on in this fashion adding sodium thiosulphate solution, then potassium iodide solution and finally edta solution.

> **16** Were your predictions in question **15** correct?

Practical 13

Determining the formulae of complex ions

REQUIREMENTS

For the colorimetric investigation each pair of students will need:

0.05 mol dm⁻³ CuSO₄ (60 cm³). Dissolve 12.5 g of CuSO₄.5H₂O in distilled water and make up to 1 dm³.

0.05 mol dm⁻³ 1,2-diaminoethane (60 cm³). Dissolve 3.0 g of H₂NCH₂CH₂NH₂ in distilled water and make up to 1 dm³.

> **CARE!**
> *Solid 1,2-diaminoethane is corrosive and its vapour is an irritant to the eyes and skin.*

9 test tubes

2 × 10 cm³ graduated pipettes or 2 burettes

Colorimeter (The suggested concentrations may require modification for the particular colorimeters used.)

For the complexometric investigation each pair of students will need:

Eye protection

0.1 mol dm⁻³ edta (disodium salt)–(80 cm³). Dissolve 33.6 g [CH₂N(CH₂COOH)CH₂COONa]₂ in distilled water and made up to 1 dm³

0.1 mol dm⁻³ Ni²⁺ salt – 80 cm³. Dissolve 39.5 g NiSO₄.(NH₄)₂SO₄.6H₂O (**harmful**) in distilled water and make up to 1 dm³.

Burette

Pipette (20 or 25 cm³)

Beaker (100 cm³)

Murexide. (Shake 0.5 g of powdered murexide with 100 cm³ of water. Allow the undissolved solid to settle and use the saturated supernatant (Prepare fresh solution daily.)

Conical flask (250 cm³)

Time required ¾ hour or 1½ hours depending on whether one or both experiments are carried out

Introduction

In determining the formula of a complex ion, we need to find the number of ligands complexing with one metal ion. This can be done by several methods, the most important of which are.

a colorimetric methods requiring measurement of the colour intensity of the complex ion as the proportion of metal ion to ligand is varied,

b titration methods involving competitive complexing.

The object of this experiment is first to investigate the formula of the copper(II)/1,2-diaminoethane complex using colorimetry, and then to investigate the formula of the nickel(II)/cdta complex using a titration method.

> **CARE!**
> *Eye protection must be worn for experiment 1 and experiment 2.*

EYE PROTECTION MUST BE WORN

> ## Experiment 1:
> ## Determining the formula of the copper(II)/1,2-diaminoethane complex by colorimetry

The formula of a complex ion can be investigated by colorimetry if there is a significant difference in colour between the simple aqueous ions and the complex. Basic ideas regarding colorimetry are discussed in the introduction to practical 17. When aqueous Cu^{2+} ions react with 1,2-diaminoethane ($H_2NCH_2CH_2NH_2$), a deeply coloured complex ion is produced. We can write an equation for this reaction as:

$$Cu^{2+}(aq) + xH_2NCH_2CH_2NH_2(aq) \rightarrow [Cu(H_2NCH_2CH_2NH_2)_x]^{2+}(aq)$$

In order to determine the formula of the complex, we must find the value of x. This can be done using the method of continuous variation described below.

Procedure

Take 9 test tubes and number them 1 to 9. Using these test tubes, make up mixtures of 0.05 mol dm⁻³ CuSO₄ and 0.05 mol dm⁻³ 1,2-diaminoethane with the volumes shown in table 1 (overleaf). Shake each tube to ensure the solutions are thoroughly mixed. Notice that each tube contains a total volume of 12 cm³.

IRRITANT
vapour from
1,2-diaminoethane solution

Test tube number	1	2	3	4	5	6	7	8	9
Vol. of 0.05 mol dm⁻³ CuSO₄/cm³	0.0	2.0	3.0	4.0	6.0	8.0	9.0	10.0	12.0
Vol. of 0.05 mol dm⁻³ 1,2-diaminoethane/cm³	12.0	10.0	9.0	8.0	6.0	4.0	3.0	2.0	0.0

Table 1

1 What is the colour of the copper(II)/1,2-diaminoethane complex ion?

2 What is the colour of the filter which would be most suitable for the experiment?

Adjust the colorimeter to obtain zero absorbance (100% transmission) when tube 1, containing only 1,2-diaminoethane solution, is placed in the colorimeter. Now measure the absorbance of the other mixtures relative to this zero reading.

3 Plot a graph of absorbance (vertical) against the volume of 0.05 mol dm⁻³ CuSO₄ (horizontal). Write the volume of 0.05 mol dm⁻³ 1,2-diaminoethane solution on the same horizontal axis as well (figure 1).

4 What are the volumes of the two solutions which, on mixing, give the maximum colour intensity?

5 In what molar proportions do Cu^{2+} and $H_2NCH_2CH_2NH_2$ react to form the complex?

6 Write an equation for the formation of the complex.

7 Draw the structural formula you would predict for the complex ion and relate this structure to that of $[Cu(NH_3)_4]^{2+}$.

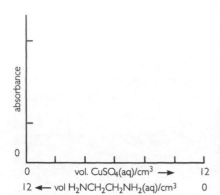

Figure 1

Experiment 2:
Determining the formula of the nickel(II)/edta complex by competitive complexing

Add 5 drops of murexide solution (figure 2) to 5 cm³ of a 0.1 mol dm⁻³ solution of a nickel(II) salt. Add edta solution to the mixture slowly until no further changes occur.

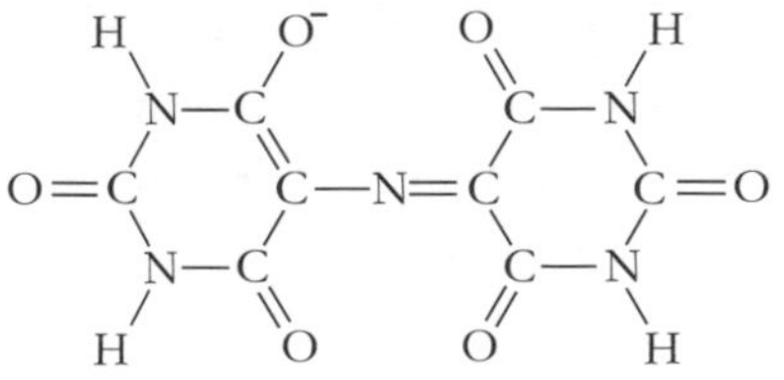

8 What are the colours of Ni^{2+} ions complexed with:
   a water, **b** murexide?

9 Explain the reactions that have occurred in terms of competitive complexing. (Remember that the final colour of the solution is due to the nickel(II)/edta complex and the non-complexed murexide.)

Figure 2
The anion ligand in murexide has the structure shown above.

The colour of the nickel(II)/murexide remains as long as there are more than enough Ni^{2+} ions for the edta, because the excess Ni^{2+} ions form a complex with murexide. As the nickel(II)/murexide complex is removed, the colour of the solution changes and the nickel(II)/edta complex forms. When all the nickel has complexed with edta, there will be no colour due to the nickel(II)/murexide complex.

So, murexide can act as an indicator in nickel(II)/edta titrations.

10 Devise a titration to determine the volume of 0.1 mol dm^{-3} edta which will just react with 20 cm^3 or 25 cm^3 of 0.1 mol dm^{-3} Ni^{2+} salt.

Discuss your suggested method with your teacher before starting a titration. (You will need to add the same proportion of murexide to nickel(II) solution as in the test tube reaction above. Mix the solutions thoroughly during the titration. Near the end-point, add the edta solution 0.5 cm^3 at a time. Titrate the solution to the same colour that you obtained in the test tube reaction.)

11 How many moles of Ni^{2+} were taken?

12 How many moles of edta reacted with this Ni^{2+}?

13 How many moles of edta react with one mole of Ni^{2+}?

14 What is the formula of the nickel(II)/edta complex?

15 Draw a diagram to represent the structure of the nickel(II)/edta complex.

Investigation

See
Investigation S11

Determining the equilibrium constant for an esterification reaction

REQUIREMENTS

Each student, or pair of students, will need:

Eye protection

Reagent bottle with tight-fitting stopper

1.0 mol dm^{-3} sodium hydroxide solution. Dissolve 40 g of sodium hydroxide pellets (**corrosive**) in distilled water and make up to 1 dm^3

Burettes containing each of the following:

glacial ethanoic (acetic) acid (**corrosive**)

ethanol (**highly flammable**)

ethyl ethanoate (ethyl acetate) (**flammable**)

3 mol dm^{-3} hydrochloric acid. Make 258 cm^3 of concentrated acid (**corrosive**) up to 1 dm^3 with distilled water

distilled water

(It is sufficient to have *one* burette containing each reagent.)

Time required   Preliminary work $\frac{1}{2}$ hour, analysis (one week later) 1 hour

Introduction

Determining the equilibrium constant K for a reaction presents some difficulties. To obtain K for a reaction, we need to find the concentration of reactants and products at equilibrium. Most methods for doing this involve removing reactant or products. This changes their concentration and, of course, disturbs the equilibrium. It is much better to use a method of measuring concentration that does not involve removing any component, such as colorimetry.

The reaction we will investigate is the esterification of ethanoic acid (acetic acid) by ethanol:

$$CH_3COOH + CH_3CH_3OH \rightleftharpoons CH_3COOCH_2CH_3 + H_2O$$
ethanoic   ethanol   ethyl ethanoate
acid

The reaction is catalysed by H$^+$ ions. The advantage of studying this particular reaction is that it is kinetically slow. So, it is possible to measure the concentration of a reactant by titration (which removes the reactant), without significantly disturbing the equilibrium in the relatively short time it takes to carry out the titration.

Known amounts of acid, alcohol and/or ester are mixed with dilute hydrochloric acid in a stoppered bottle. The mixture is set aside for at least a week so as to reach equilibrium at room temperature. The mixture is then titrated with alkali in order to find the total amount of acid present. After allowing for the presence of the hydrochloric acid catalyst, the amount of ethanoic acid present at equilibrium can be calculated. From this the amounts of the other reagents can be calculated, and hence a value for the equilibrium constant can be found.

Procedure

Preliminary

CARE!
Eye protection must be worn throughout.

Burettes are set up in the laboratory containing the following:

- ethyl ethanoate (ethyl acetate)
- pure ('glacial') ethanoic acid (**CARE Corrosive**)
- approximately 3 mol dm^{-3} HCl

IRRITANT
Hydrochloric acid

EYE PROTECTION MUST BE WORN

HIGHLY FLAMMABLE
Ethanol
Ethyl ethanoate

CORROSIVE
Glacial ethanoic acid

- ethanol
- distilled water

You will be asked to make up one of the mixtures in table 1 in a reagent bottle. Before starting, make sure the reagent bottle has a well-fitting stopper. Run the liquids into the reagent bottle from the burettes, and stopper immediately to prevent evaporation. Shake well, then allow the bottle to stand at room temperature for a week, to allow the mixture to reach equilibrium.

Notice that the total volume in each experiment is 10 cm^3.

Experiment number	HCl/cm³	Water/cm³	Ethyl ethanoate/cm³	Ethanoic acid/cm³	Ethanol /cm³
1	5	0	5	0	0
2	5	1	4	0	0
3	5	2	3	0	0
4	5	3	2	0	0
5	5	0	4	0	1
6	5	0	4	1	0
7	5	0	0	1	4
8	5	0	0	2	3

Table 1

CORROSIVE
Sodium hydroxide solution

After one week

Titrate the whole of the mixture in the bottle with 1.0 mol dm^{-3} sodium hydroxide solution, using phenolphthalein as indicator.

In order to find the exact concentration of the HCl catalyst, titrate 5 cm^3 of the approximately 3 mol dm^{-3} HCl with 1.0 mol dm^{-3} NaOH.

Finally, weigh 5 cm^3 of each of the liquids used to make up your mixture (including the HCl).

Finding the equilibrium constant

1 How many moles of ethyl ethanoate were there in your *original* mixture (i.e. before any reaction had occurred)?

2 How many moles of ethanoic acid were there in your original mixture?

3 How many moles of ethanol were there in your original mixture?

4 How many moles of water were there in your original mixture? (Remember to take into account the water present in the dilute HCl. You can find the mass of this by deducting the mass of pure HCl, found by titration, from the mass of 5 cm^3 of 3 mol dm^{-3} HCl.)

5 How many moles of ethanoic acid were there in the mixture *at equilibrium*? (This can be found from the volume of 1.0 mol dm^{-3} NaOH needed to titrate the mixture, after subtracting the volume of NaOH needed to titrate 5 cm^3 of approximately 3 mol dm^{-3} HCl.)

6 How many moles of ethanol were there in the mixture *at equilibrium*? (This can be found from your answers to questions 2 and 5. If the number of moles of ethanoic acid *changes* by x from the original mixture to the equilibrium, the number of moles of ethanol will change by the same amount.)

7 How many moles of:
a ethyl ethanoate,
b water,
were there in the mixture at equilibrium?

(From the equation for the reaction, you should realise that if the number of moles of ethanoic acid and ethanol *increase* by x from the original mixture to the equilibrium, then the ethyl ethanoate and water will *decrease* by the same amount.)

8 Work out the *concentrations* of water, ethyl ethanoate, ethanol and ethanoic acid in the mixture at equilibrium, using your answers to questions 5 to 7 and the fact that the total volume of the reaction mixture was 10 cm^3.

9 What is the equilibrium constant for this reaction?

10 Compare your result with those obtained by other members of the group who started with different mixtures. Does the value of the equilibrium constant depend on the starting concentration of the reactants?

11 ΔH for this reaction is $+17.5 \text{ kJ mol}^{-1}$. Would you expect the value of K_c to be greater or smaller at $80\,^{\circ}\text{C}$ than at room temperature?

12 The yield of ester formed in the reaction between ethanoic acid and ethanol is considerably increased if concentrated sulphuric acid is added to the reactants. Suggest a reason for this.

Investigation
See
Investigation L4

Practical 15

Determining the order of a reaction

REQUIREMENTS

Each pair of students will need:

Eye protection

Burette and stand

Beaker (1 dm³)

Measuring cylinder (500 cm³)

Measuring cylinder (25 or 50 cm³)

Measuring cylinder (10 cm³)

Stirring rod

Pipette (10 cm³) and safety filler

Clock or watch with seconds hand

Graph paper

Small funnel

2 small beakers

Approximately 0.1 mol dm⁻³ H_2O_2(30 cm³)

0.05 mol dm⁻³ $Na_2S_2O_3$ (100 cm³)

1.0 mol dm⁻³ H_2SO_4 (75 cm³) (**irritant**)

1.0 mol dm⁻³ KI (45 cm³)

Starch solution (2 cm³) (see Practical 4)

Time required   1–1½ hours

Introduction

For the reaction:

$$xA + yB \longrightarrow \text{products,}$$

experiments show that the reaction rate can be related to the concentrations of A and B by the equation:

$$\text{Rate} = k[A]^m[B]^n$$

This expression is know as the **rate equation** or **rate law** for the reaction. m and n are constants whose values are usually 0, 1 or 2 in most cases, and k is the **rate constant** for the reaction.

The index m is known as **the order of the reaction with respect to A**, and n is the order of the reaction with respect to B. The **overall order** of the reaction is $(m + n)$.

The reaction we shall be studying involves hydrogen peroxide and iodide ions in acid solution.

$$H_2O_2(aq) + 2I^-(aq) + 2H^+(aq) \longrightarrow 2H_2O(l) + I_2(aq)$$

The rate equation for this reaction can be written as:

$$\text{Rate} = k[H_2O_2]^\alpha[I^-]^\beta[H^+]^\gamma$$

The order of the reaction with respect to one reactant can be investigated by having the other reactants in large excess so that their concentrations are effectively constant. For example, in this experiment, the order of the reaction with respect to H_2O_2 is investigated by using much larger concentrations of I^- and H^+.

Under these circumstances the reaction rate can be expressed as:

$$\text{Rate} = k'[H_2O_2]^n$$

k' is a modified rate constant which includes the constant concentrations of I^- and H^+.

Principle

The object of this experiment is to determine the order with respect to H_2O_2 for the reaction discussed above.

Hydrogen peroxide is allowed to react with an acidified solution of potassium iodide forming iodine.

$$H_2O_2(aq) + 2I^-(aq) + 2H^+(aq) \longrightarrow 2H_2O(l) + I_2(aq)$$

Small quantities of starch and sodium thiosulphate are also present. As the iodine is produced, it reacts with thiosulphate and is converted back to iodide ions:

$$I_2(aq) + 2S_2O_3^{2-}(aq) \longrightarrow 2I^-(aq) + S_4O_6^{2-}(aq)$$

When the iodine produced in the reaction is in excess of the sodium thiosulphate, a blue colour suddenly appears as the iodine reacts with starch.

From the amount of $S_2O_3^{2-}$ added, we can calculate the amount of I_2 produced by the time the blue colour appears and hence the amount of H_2O_2 used up.

Knowing the original amount of H_2O_2, we can calculate $[H_2O_2]$ at the time the blue colour appears. The values of $[H_2O_2]$ at different times can then be used to find the order of reaction with respect to H_2O_2.

Procedure

IRRITANT
Dilute sulphuric acid

EYE PROTECTION MUST BE WORN

CARE!
Eye protection must be worn.

Fill a burette with 0.05 mol dm^{-3} Na$_2$S$_2$O$_3$(aq).

Put 450 cm^3 of distilled water in a 1 dm^3 beaker and add 25 cm^3 of 1.0 mol dm^{-3} H$_2$SO$_4$, 1 cm^3 of starch solution and 15 cm^3 of 1.0 mol dm^{-3} KI. Finally, add 2 cm^3 of 0.05 mol dm^{-3} S$_2$O$_3^{2-}$(aq) from the burette. Now, start the reaction by rapidly adding 10 cm^3 of approximately 0.1 mol dm^{-3} H$_2$O$_2$ from a pipette **using a safety filler**. Stir during this addition. (Start timing when half of the H$_2$O$_2$ has been added.)

When the I$_2$ produced in the reaction is in excess of the added S$_2$O$_3^{2-}$, a blue colour will suddenly appear. Quickly, note the time, add a further 2 cm^3 of S$_2$O$_3^{2-}$(aq) and the blue colour will disappear.

Note the time again when the blue colour reappears and add another 2 cm^3 of S$_2$O$_3^{2-}$(aq). Continue in this manner until 8–10 readings have been obtained.

Finally, determine the exact concentration of the H$_2$O$_2$ as follows. Pipette 10 cm^3 of approximately 0.1 mol dm^{-3} H$_2$O$_2$ into a conical flask **using a safety filler**. Then, add 25 cm^3 of 1.0 mol dm^{-3} H$_2$SO$_4$ and 15 cm^3 of 1.0 mol dm^{-3} KI and titrate this mixture against the 0.05 mol dm^{-3} S$_2$O$_3^{2-}$(aq) using starch as indicator.

1 Why must the other reactants (e.g. KI and H$_2$SO$_4$) be in large excess compared with H$_2$O$_2$?

2 Why is the concentration of I$^-$ constant throughout the whole experiment? (**Hint.** Look closely at the equations for the reactions involved.)

3 Why does the time interval between appearances of the blue colour become longer?

4 Why is it important to stir during the addition of the H$_2$O$_2$?

5 If the H$_2$O$_2$ solution is exactly of 0.1 mol dm^{-3} and the S$_2$O$_3^{2-}$ solution is exactly 0.05 mol dm^{-3} then:

10 cm^3 of 0.1 mol dm^{-3} H$_2$O$_2$ will just react with 40 cm^3 of 0.05 mol dm^{-3} S$_2$O$_3^{2-}$ during titration. Explain why this is.

6 From the amount of S$_2$O$_3^{2-}$ added, we can calculate the amount of I$_2$ produced by the time the blue colour appears and hence the amount of H$_2$O$_2$ used up. Knowing the original amount of H$_2$O$_2$, we can then calculate the concentration of H$_2$O$_2$ at different times.

The concentration of H_2O_2 is most conveniently expressed in terms of the volume of 0.05 mol dm^{-3} Na$_2$S$_2$O$_3$ added.

For example, suppose the H_2O_2 is exactly 0.1 mol dm^{-3}. Its initial concentration would then be equivalent to 40 cm^3 of 0.05 mol dm^{-3} S$_2$O$_3^{2-}$. Suppose the blue colour first appears after x seconds, and appears a second time after y seconds. We can then say:

At $t = 0$ s, 40 cm^3 0.05 mol dm^{-3} S$_2$O$_3^{2-}$(aq) $\propto$ [H_2O_2];

at $t = x$ s, when blue colour first appears,

$(40 - 2) = 38$ cm^3 0.05 mol dm^{-3} S$_2$O$_3^{2-}$(aq) $\propto$ [H_2O_2];

at $t = y$ s, when blue colour appears a second time,

$(40 - 4) = 36$ cm^3 0.05 mol dm^{-3} S$_2$O$_3^{2-}$(aq) $\propto$ [H_2O_2]; etc.

$\Rightarrow$ At time, $t = 0$ s, [H_2O_2] $\propto 40$;

at time, $t = x$ s, [H_2O_2] $\propto 38$;

at time $t = y$ s, [H_2O_2] $\propto 36$; etc.

Record your results in a table similar to table 1. Remember to use your own value for the volume of S$_2$O$_3^{2-}$ needed to titrate 10 cm^3 of the approximately 0.1 mol dm^{-3} H_2O_2. This is unlikely to be exactly 40 cm^3.

Vol. of 0.05 mol dm^{-3} S$_2$O$_3^{2-}$ added/cm^3	Vol. of 0.05 mol dm^{-3} S$_2$O$_3^{2-}\propto$ [H_2O_2]/cm^3	Time at which blue colour appears/s
0	40	0
2	38	x
4	36	y

Table 1

7 If the order of the reaction with respect to H_2O_2 is zero, then [H_2O_2] will not affect the rate of the equation. In other words, the rate of reaction will be constant, i.e.

Rate $= k$

If the rate is first order with respect to H_2O_2, then:

Rate $= k$[H_2O_2]

What is the rate equation if the reaction is second order with respect to H_2O_2?

8 Plot a graph of [H_2O_2] using values in column 2 of table 1 (vertically) against time at which the blue colour appears (horizontally).

9 Use your graph from question 8 to explore whether the reaction is zero order, first order or second order with respect to H_2O_2. Remember that the gradient of the graph at any one point will be a measure of the reaction rate at the relevant time, i.e.

$$\text{reaction rate} = \frac{\text{change in concentration}}{\text{time taken}}$$

Investigation

See
Investigation L7

Practical 16

Investigating catalysis

REQUIREMENTS

Each student, or pair of students, will need:

Eye protection

Rack plus 1 boiling tube and 2 test tubes

0.2 mol dm^{-3} KI (40 cm^3)

0.1 mol dm^{-3} Na$_2$S$_2$O$_3$ (40 cm^3)

0.2% starch solution (20 cm^3)

Saturated K$_2$S$_2$O$_8$(aq) (80 cm^3) (**oxidising solid**)

0.1 mol dm^{-3} aqueous solutions of the following cations:

Co^{2+} (Co^{2+} salt is **toxic**), Cu^{2+}, Fe^{2+}, Fe^{3+}, Mg^{2+}, Zn^{2+}

0.1 mol dm^{-3} NaOH (10 cm^3) (**irritant**)

2.0 mol dm^{-3} H$_2$O$_2$ (20 cm^3) (**irritant**)

0.5 mol dm^{-3} potassium sodium tartrate (Rochelle salt) (10 cm^3)

Conical flask (100 cm^3)

Clock or watch with seconds hand

Measuring cylinder (10 cm^3)

Measuring cylinder (25 cm^3)

Bunsen, tripod and gauze

Time required   Experiment 1: 30 minutes

Experiment 2: 30 minutes

Introduction

Catalysts are substances that alter the rate of chemical reactions without any overall chemical change to themselves.

Although catalysts are *not* used up in reactions, they take part by forming intermediates as the reactants are changed into the products.

In this practical, you will be studying the effects of various metal ions as catalysts in aqueous solution and investigating the way in which they can take part in the reaction.

Principle

EYE PROTECTION MUST BE WORN

> **CARE!**
> *Eye protection must be worn in all these experiments.*

Experiment 1:
Studying the catalysis of the reaction between iodide and peroxodisulphate(VI) ions by metal ions

Iodide ions are oxidised to iodine by peroxodisulphate(VI) ions in a relatively slow reaction.

$$S_2O_8^{2-}(aq) + 2I^-(aq) \rightarrow 2SO_4^{2-}(aq) + I_2(aq) \qquad \text{(slow)}$$

In the presence of starch, iodine forms a dark blue solution. Some metal ions will catalyse this reaction.

A neat way to measure the reaction rate is to add a fixed amount of sodium thiosulphate to the reaction mixture. This reacts rapidly with the iodine formed in the reaction and converts it back to iodide.

$$I_2(aq) + 2S_2O_3^{2-}(aq) \rightarrow 2I^-(aq) + S_4O_6^{2-}(aq) \qquad \text{(fast)}$$

When all the thiosulphate is used up, the iodine produced reacts with starch to give a blue colour. Now,

$$\text{reaction rate} = \frac{\text{change in concentration of } S_2O_8^{2-}}{\text{time taken for blue colour to appear}}$$

But, the change in concentration of $S_2O_8^{2-}$ is the same in all experiments. So:

$$\text{reaction rate} \propto \frac{1}{\text{time taken for blue colour to appear}}$$

The effects of metal ions as catalysts can be compared by comparing the reaction times with and without the different metal ions.

Procedure

Put 10 cm^3 of 0.2 mol dm^{-3} potassium iodide, 10 cm^3 of 0.1 mol dm^{-3} sodium thiosulphate and 5 cm^3 of 0.2% starch solution in a 100 cm^3 conical flask.

Measure out 20 cm^3 of saturated potassium peroxodisulphate(VI) into a boiling tube. Add this rapidly to the mixture in the flask, swirl and start timing the reaction. Note the time taken (to the nearest second) for the blue colour to appear.

Now repeat the experiment, but this time add 3 drops of a 0.1 mol dm^{-3} solution of one of the metal ions listed below to the conical flask before adding the peroxodisulphate(VI) solution:

Cu^{2+}, Fe^{2+}, Fe^{3+}, Mg^{2+}, Zn^{2+}.

1   Make a clear table of your results. (If you have not carried out the experiment for each of the metal ions listed, obtain these results from other groups.)

2   Which metal ions catalyse the $I^-/S_2O_8^{2-}$ reaction?

3   What type of reaction takes place between I^- and $S_2O_8^{2-}$?

4   Which type of metal ions frequently act as catalysts?

5   Try to suggest a mechanism by which certain metal ions can catalyse this reaction.

Experiment 2:

Studying the decomposition of hydrogen peroxide with transition metal ions

A Catalysis by Fe^{3+}

EYE PROTECTION
MUST BE WORN

IRRITANT
Hydrogen peroxide
solution
Sodium hydroxide
solution

Put 5 cm^3 of 2 mol dm^{-3} hydrogen peroxide (H_2O_2) in each of two test tubes and add 5 cm^3 of 0.1 mol dm^{-3} sodium hydroxide to each.

Now add 3 drops of a 0.1 mol dm^{-3} solution of Fe^{3+}(aq) to one of the tubes. Compare the rates of production of gas in the two tubes.

6   Write an equation for the decomposition of hydrogen peroxide to water and oxygen.

7   How does the reaction rate compare in the two tubes?

8   The decomposition of H_2O_2 can be written as two half-equations:

$$H_2O_2 \rightarrow O_2 + 2H^+ + 2e^-$$
$$H_2O_2 + 2H^+ + 2e^- \rightarrow 2H_2O$$

Suggest an explanation for the different reaction rates in the two tubes.

IRRITANT
Hydrogen peroxide solution

EYE PROTECTION MUST BE WORN

TOXIC
Co^{2+} salt solution

B Catalysis by Co^{2+}

Put 10 cm^3 of 0.5 mol dm^{-3} potassium sodium tartrate and 10 cm^3 of 2 mol dm^{-3} H$_2$O$_2$ in a 100 cm^3 conical flask.

Heat the mixture until it is nearly boiling.

Note any signs of reaction by the evolution of gas.

Now add a little 0.1 mol dm^{-3} Co^{2+} salt until the solution has a definite pink colour.

9   What slowly happens?

10 When is the evolution of gas most vigorous?

11 Bearing in mind that Co^{2+} salts are pink/red and Co^{3+} salts are green, suggest a mechanism for the catalysis of the reaction by cobalt ions. (Remember that the decomposition of H$_2$O$_2$ can be considered as two half-equations as above.)

Using colorimetry to find the order of the reaction between bromine and methanoic acid

REQUIREMENTS

Each pair of students will need:

Eye protection

0.1 mol dm⁻³ bromine (25 cm³) (**toxic and corrosive**). Dissolve 16 g (5 cm³) of Br_2 in distilled water and make up to 1 dm³

1.0 mol dm⁻³ methanoic acid (25 cm³) (**irritant**). Dissolve 46 g (37.7 cm³) of HCOOH in distilled water and make up to 1 dm³

> ### CARE!
> *Both methanoic acid and bromine are corrosive, fuming liquids capable of causing serious burns. Their solutions should be prepared in a fume cupboard, and protective gloves should be worn.*

(The concentrations of these two solutions may need modification with certain colorimeters.)

Colorimeter with blue, green or turquoise filter

Distilled water (10 cm³)

2 measuring cylinders (25 or 50 cm³)

1 boiling tube

2 matched thin-walled (soda) test tubes for use with the colorimeter

Stop clock or watch reading in seconds

Time required 1 hour

Introduction

In this practical, the technique of colorimetry is introduced and then used to investigate the reaction between bromine and methanoic acid. Colorimetry can be used to determine the concentration of any coloured substance. It is particularly useful in the study of reaction rates, where the concentration of a coloured substance is constantly changing.

In a colorimeter, a narrow beam of light passes through the solution under test towards a sensitive photocell (figure 1). In most colorimeters, it is possible to select the most appropriate colour (wavelength) of light by choosing a particular filter or by adjusting a diffraction grating.

The current generated in the photocell depends on the intensity of light transmitted by the solution which in turn depends upon the concentration of the coloured solution under test. The current generated in the photocell will be greatest when the light transmitted by the coloured solution is greatest, i.e. when the coloured solution is least concentrated. Normally, the meter is not calibrated to show the light transmitted but the light absorbed (**absorbance**) which is proportional to the concentration of the coloured solution.

Absorbance ∝ concentration of coloured species

In the following experiment, the coloured species is bromine, so absorbance ∝ $[Br_2]$.

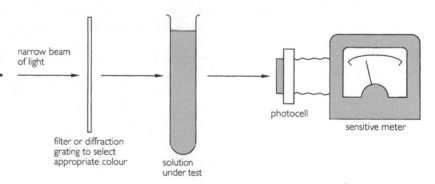

narrow beam of light

filter or diffraction grating to select appropriate colour

solution under test

photocell

sensitive meter

Figure 1
A simplified diagram of a colorimeter.

Principle

The reaction under investigation is:

$$Br_2(aq) + HCOOH(aq) \rightarrow 2Br^-(aq) + 2H^+(aq) + CO_2(g)$$

Using a concentration of methanoic acid 10 times larger than that of bromine, we can assume that the concentration of methanoic acid is constant throughout the experiment. This allows us to see how the concentration of bromine affects the reaction rate. If the reaction is zero order with respect to bromine,

$$\frac{-d[Br_2]}{dt} = k_0$$

$-d[Br_2]/dt$ represents the reaction rate in terms of the rate of change of concentration of bromine, and k_0 is the rate constant for a zero order reaction. Integrating this equation gives:

$$-[Br_2] = k_0t + constant \tag{1}$$

Thus a graph of $[Br_2]$ (or absorbance) against t (time) should give a straight line.

If the reaction is first order with respect to bromine,

$$\frac{-d[Br_2]}{dt} = k_1[Br_2]$$

where k_1 is the rate constant for a first order reaction. Integration of this equation gives:

$$-\ln[Br_2] = k_1t + constant \tag{2}$$

$-\ln[Br_2]$ is minus the logarithm to base e of the concentration of bromine.

Thus, a graph of $\ln[Br_2]$ (or ln absorbance) against t (time) should give a straight line.

If the reaction is second order with respect to bromine,

$$\frac{-d[Br_2]}{dt} = k_2[Br_2]^2$$

where k_2 is the rate constant for a second order reaction. Integration of this equation gives:

$$\frac{1}{[Br_2]} = k_2t + constant \tag{3}$$

Thus a graph of $1/[Br_2]$ (or the reciprocal of the absorbance) against t (time) should give a straight line.

By plotting three graphs, one for absorbance against time, one for ln(absorbance) against time and a third for the reciprocal of absorbance against time, we can determine the order of reaction with respect to bromine.

Procedure

EYE PROTECTION MUST BE WORN

> **CARE!**
> *Eye protection must be worn.*

Turn the sensitivity controls of the colorimeter to a minimum and insert a blue or green filter. Switch on the colorimeter and allow five minutes for it to warm up.

CORROSIVE
Bromine solution

TOXIC
Bromine solution

IRRITANT
Methanoic acid

Insert a thin-walled test tube containing water into the colorimeter and cover it with a cap. Adjust the sensitivity (using the higher sensitivity controls) to give zero absorbance (i.e. 100% transmission). Now, mix 10 cm^3 of 1.0 mol dm^{-3} methanoic acid with an equal volume of 0.1 mol dm^{-3} bromine in a boiling tube and start the stop watch. Shake the mixture gently, transfer some of it to a colorimeter tube and read the absorbance on the colorimeter after 15 seconds, 30 seconds, 45 seconds, 60 seconds, etc. Nine or ten readings should be sufficient.

1   What are the advantages of colorimetry over titration analysis in rate experiments such as this?

2   Why is it necessary to use carefully matched tubes in the colorimeter?

3   Why is a blue or green filter chosen in this experiment? (**Hint**: as the bromine is used up and its orange colour disappears, you want the difference in absorbance to be as large as possible.)

4   Tabulate your results. The columns of your table should show time, absorbance, ln(absorbance) and reciprocal of absorbance.

5   Using the same axes (but with different vertical scales), plot graphs of:

   a   absorbance against time,
   b   ln(absorbance) against time,
   c   reciprocal of absorbance against time.

6   Which graph is nearest to a straight line?

7   What is the order of reaction with respect to bromine?

8   Why is the graph for the correct order not absolutely straight even when there are no experimental errors? (**Hint**: What assumption has been made which is not wholly true?)

9   Look at the equations numbered (1), (2) and (3) in the section headed 'Principle'.
   Using the appropriate rate equation, it is possible to obtain a value for the rate constant for the reaction.

   a   Which equation relates to the order of the reaction with respect to bromine?
   b   Notice that the graph for this equation will have a gradient equal to k, the rate constant. Calculate a value for the rate constant and show its units.

Investigation
See
Investigation L8

Practical 18

Determining the activation energy of the reaction between bromide and bromate(V) ions

REQUIREMENTS

Each pair of students will need:

Eye protection

0.01 mol dm^{-3} phenol (70 cm^3). Dissolve 0.94 g of phenol in distilled water and make up to 1 dm^3

> **CARE!**
> *Solid phenol is toxic and corrosive. Avoid skin contact and wear protective gloves when preparing the solution.*

Br$^-$/BrO$_3^-$ solution (0.1 mol dm^{-3} w.r.t. potassium bromide, KBr, and 0.02 mol dm^{-3} w.r.t. potassium bromate(V), KBrO$_3$ (70 cm^3). Dissolve 11.90 g of KBr and 3.34 g of KBrO$_3$ (**oxidising solid**) in distilled water and make up to 1 dm^3

0.05 mol dm^{-3} H$_2$SO$_4$ (35 cm^3)

Methyl red indicator (28 drops)

Large beaker (1 dm^3 or 500 cm^3)

Thermometer (0–100 °C)

2 boiling tubes

Measuring cylinder (10 cm^3 or 20 cm^3)

Bunsen burner

Tripod and gauze

Clock or watch with seconds hand

Time required   1 hour

Introduction

During a reaction, bonds are first broken, and others are then formed. Energy is required to break certain bonds and start this process, whether the overall reaction is exothermic or endothermic. Particles do not always react when they collide because they may not possess sufficient energy for the appropriate bonds to break.

A reaction will only occur if the colliding particles possess more than a certain minimum amount of energy known as the **activation energy**, E_A. During the 1930s, Zartmann, Ko and others showed that the distribution of kinetic energies amongst the particles of a liquid or gas was similar to that shown in figure 1.

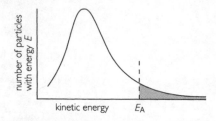

Figure 1

Essentially, the curve is a histogram showing the number of particles within each small range of kinetic energy. So, the area beneath the curve is proportional to the total number of particles in that energy range.

Consequently, the number of particles capable of reacting, with energy greater than the activation energy, E_A, is proportional to the shaded area beneath the curve. Hence the *fraction* of particles with energy greater than E_A is given by the ratio:

$$\frac{\text{(shaded area beneath curve)}}{\text{(total area beneath curve)}}$$

Using the kinetic theory and probability theory, Maxwell and Boltzmann showed that the fraction of molecules with energy greater than E_A was given by $e^{-E_A/RT}$. R is the gas constant, T is the absolute temperature and e is the exponential function.

This suggests that at a given temperature, T:

Reaction rate $\propto e^{-E_A/RT}$

But as k, the rate constant for a reaction, is a measure of the reaction rate, we can write:

$k \propto e^{-E_A/RT}$

$\Rightarrow k = Ae^{-E_A/RT}$

This last expression is called the **Arrhenius equation**, because it was first predicted by the Swedish chemist Svante Arrhenius in 1889.

Principle

The object of this experiment is to obtain E_A for the reaction between Br^- and BrO_3^- in acid solution.

$$5Br^-(aq) + BrO_3^-(aq) + 6H^+(aq) \rightarrow 3Br_2(aq) + 3H_2O(l)$$

The time, t, for the reaction to proceed to the same small extent at different temperatures is found. This is done by adding a fixed amount of phenol and a small amount of methyl red indicator to the reaction mixture.

The bromine produced during the reaction reacts very rapidly with phenol (forming tribromophenol). As soon as all the phenol is consumed, any further bromine bleaches the indicator immediately. Now,

$$k \propto \text{reaction rate} = \frac{\text{change in concentration}}{\text{time taken}},$$

but as the change in concentration in this experiment is the same at each temperature,

$$k \propto \frac{1}{\text{time for methyl red to be bleached}}$$

$$\therefore \quad k = \frac{c}{\text{time for methyl red to be bleached}}$$

$$= \frac{c}{t}$$

where c is a constant and t is the time taken to bleach the methyl red. Hence, $c/t = Ae^{-E_A/RT}$ and if we take logs to base e:

$$\ln\left(\frac{c}{t}\right) = \ln A + \ln e^{-E_A/RT}$$

$$\Rightarrow \ln c - \ln t = \ln A - \frac{E_A}{R} \cdot \frac{1}{T}$$

$$\Rightarrow \ln t = \ln c - \ln A + \frac{E_A}{R} \cdot \frac{1}{T}$$

$\ln c$ and $\ln A$ are constants. R, the gas constant, equals $8.3 \text{ J K}^{-1} \text{ mol}^{-1}$ and E_A is assumed to be constant. So a graph of $\ln t$ against $1/T$ has a gradient of E_A/R.

Procedure

**EYE PROTECTION
MUST BE WORN**

> **CARE!**
> *Eye protection must be worn.*

Work in pairs.
Use a measuring cylinder to put 10 cm^3 of 0.01 mol dm^{-3} phenol and 10 cm^3 of the bromide/bromate(V) solution into a boiling tube. Then add 4 drops of methyl red indicator. In a second boiling tube, put 5 cm^3 of 0.5 mol dm^{-3} H_2SO_4.

Fill a 1 dm³ beaker with water and warm it to about 75 °C. Adjust the heating to keep the temperature of the water steady.

Immerse the two boiling tubes in the water and when their contents reach the water temperature (±1 °C), mix the contents of the tubes. Time the reaction until the colour of the methyl red disappears.

Repeat the experiment at about 65 °C, 55 °C, 45 °C, 35 °C, 25 °C and 15 °C.

1 Arrange your results in a table as below.

Temperature /°C	Temperature /K	$(1/T)$ /K^{-1}	Time taken to bleach methyl red, t/s	ln t

2 Why does the reaction not start until the contents of the boiling tubes are mixed?

3 Write an equation for the reaction between bromine and phenol.

4 What function does the methyl red play in the experiment? (**Hint**: it is not acting as an indicator in the accepted sense.)

5 Why is it unsatisfactory to measure the reaction rate at temperatures above 75 °C?

6 Plot a graph of ln t (vertically) against $1/T$ (horizontally).

7 Measure the gradient of this graph and obtain the value of E_A. ($R = 8.3$ J K^{-1} mol^{-1}.) Show the units for E_A.

8 Is the value of E_A positive or negative? What does this signify?

9 How is E_A related to the enthalpy change for the forward reaction, ΔH_r? Draw a simple energy diagram to make your answer clear. Draw arrows to represent E_A and ΔH_r on your diagram.

Investigation

See
Investigations L7
and L8

A practical study of the third period

REQUIREMENTS

Eye protection

Samples of elements from period 3

Because of the hazardous nature of sodium (**highly flammable**), phosphorus (**toxic**) and chlorine (**toxic**), it is best for the teacher to demonstrate these elements. It is important to avoid confusion between phosphorus (stored under water) and sodium (stored under oil).Ideally, phosphorus and sodium should not be in the laboratory at the same time.

Simple apparatus to test electrical conductivity

1 rack + 4 test tubes

Full-range indicator paper

Samples of the following oxides: Na_2O (or NaOH) (**corrosive**), MgO, Al_2O_3, SiO_2, P_2O_5 (**corrosive**)

Access to SO_2 cylinder

Dilute hydrochloric acid (**irritant**)
Dilute sodium hydroxide solution (**corrosive**)

Samples of the following chlorides: NaCl, $MgCl_2$, $AlCl_3$, PCl_3, SCl_2 (or S_2Cl_2)

$AlCl_3$, PCl_3, SCl_2 and S_2Cl_2 are all **corrosive**

Bunsen burner

Time required   2 hours

Introduction

The periodic table provides a very important unifying pattern to the study of chemistry. The intention of this practical is to study some of the trends in properties across the third period of the periodic table.

A   Patterns in the properties of elements

The properties of the elements show a repeating pattern with increasing atomic number. The most obvious pattern is the steady change from metals on the left to non-metals on the right of each period.

Procedure

EYE PROTECTION MUST BE WORN

> **CARE!**
> *Eye protection must be worn throughout this practical.*

Examine samples of the elements sodium to argon in period 3. Test the electrical conductivity of those elements for which the results are not given in table 1.

1   Copy and complete table 1. You will have to consult a data book, or Section 4.7 in *Chemistry in Context*, Fifth Edition, for boiling point values.

	Na	Mg	Al	Si	P	S	Cl	Ar
Atomic number								
Physical state and appearance								
Boiling point/°C								
Conductivity at room temperature	good				poor		poor	poor
Structure (giant metallic, giant molecular or simple molecular)								
Type of element (metal, non-metal or metalloid)								

Table 1
The elements of period 3

TOXIC
Chlorine
White
phosphorus

FLAMMABLE
Sodium
Magnesium
Phosphorus

CORROSIVE
Sodium

2   How do the boiling points of elements vary across the period from sodium to argon? How are the boiling points related to the structure of the elements?

3   Describe the changes in:

   a the type of elements across period 3,
   b the structure of elements across period 3.

You should know quite a lot about the properties of these compounds already.

4   Copy out table 2, and complete the first three rows.

Oxide formula	Na_2O	MgO	Al_2O_3	SiO_2	P_2O_5	SO_2	Cl_2O
State at room temp.							(g)
Appearance							yellow-red gas
Volatility							high
Conductivity of molten oxide	good	good	good	poor	poor	poor	poor
Solubility in water							dissolves readily
pH of solution in water							2
Classification of oxide (acidic, basic or amphoteric)							acidic
Structure of oxide (simple molecular, giant molecular, giant ionic)							simple molecular

Table 2
Properties of the oxides in period 3

USE A FUME CUPBOARD

EYE PROTECTION MUST BE WORN

TOXIC
Sulphur dioxide

CORROSIVE
Sodium oxide
Phosphorus(V) oxide
Sodium hydroxide solid

WEAR PROTECTIVE GLOVES

CARE!
Avoid skin contact when using Na_2O and P_2O_5.

Test the solubility of each oxide in water. Add a **very small** measure of each solid to about 3 cm³ of distilled water and shake thoroughly. (In the case of sulphur dioxide, bubble the gas through 3 cm³ of water in a **fume cupboard** for a few seconds.)

If Na_2O is not available, use sodium hydroxide (NaOH) (**CARE Corrosive. Wear protective gloves.**) Some oxides will dissolve easily. Others will not dissolve at all. Test the pH of the solution obtained from each oxide using full-range indicator paper. Record your results in table 2.

5   Which of the oxides of period 3 elements:

   a form acidic solutions with water,
   b form alkaline solutions with water,
   c are insoluble in water?

6   Write equations for the reactions of the soluble oxides with water.

If an oxide is insoluble in water, its reactions with acids and alkalis can be used to decide its acid–base character. If an oxide dissolves in acid, it must have reacted with it. The oxide can therefore be classified as basic. If the oxide dissolves in alkali, it can be described as acidic. If the insoluble oxide dissolves in both acids and alkalis, it is both basic and acidic. The adjective 'amphoteric' (from a Greek word meaning 'both') is used to describe these oxides.

CORROSIVE
Sodium hydroxide
solution

IRRITANT
Hydrochloric acid

Test the solubility of the insoluble oxides in dilute hydrochloric acid and then in dilute sodium hydroxide solution. Remember to use **very small** measures of solid.

7 Write equations for any reactions of the insoluble oxides:

a with hydrochloric acid,
b with sodium hydroxide solution.

8 Complete the last two lines in table 2.

9 Describe the following patterns in the properties of the oxides across period 3:

a their state,
b their character (acidic/amphoteric/basic),
c their structure.

C Patterns in the properties of chlorides

Examine samples of the chlorides of period 3 elements.

10 Copy out table 3 and complete the first two rows. (You will **not** be expected to test silicon tetrachloride yourself. The results for this are already inserted.)

Element	Na	Mg	Al	Si	P	S
Formula of chloride				$SiCl_4$		
Appearance and state of chloride				colourless liquid		
Volatility of chloride				high		
Action of water on chloride				very vigorous reaction, HCl fumes evolved		
pH of solution of chloride in water				3		
Structure of chloride				simple molecular		

Table 3
Properties of the chlorides in period 3

CORROSIVE
Aluminium chloride
Phosphorus chlorides
Sulphur chlorides

**EYE PROTECTION
MUST BE WORN**

**USE A FUME
CUPBOARD**

CARE!
Take great care with the chlorides of aluminium, phosphorus and sulphur. Work in a fume cupboard and wear eye protection.

Working in a fume cupboard, warm separate **small** samples of the chlorides gently with a bunsen.

Investigate the relative volatility of the chlorides and put your results in table 3.

Investigate the effect of water on each chloride by adding a **small** quantity to about 3 cm^3 of distilled water in a test tube.

CARE!

Eye protection is essential. Some of the chlorides react very vigorously with water.

Test the pH of the mixture obtained using full-range indicator paper, then complete table 3.

11 Explain, with equations, the action of sodium chloride, aluminium chloride and phosphorus chloride with water.

12 Describe the patterns across period 3 in:

   a the formula of the chlorides,
   b the state of the chlorides,
   c the pH of the aqueous chloride solutions,
   d the structure of the chlorides.

Practical 20

A practical study of some Group II elements

REQUIREMENTS

Each student, or pair of students, will require:

Eye protection

Hard-glass test tubes (8)

Stopper to fit tubes

Test tube holders

Angled glass bend with bung to fit test tube

Beaker (400 cm³)

Funnel

Universal indicator solution

Indicator paper

Filter paper

Splints

Emery paper

Magnesium ribbon (**highly flammable**)

Magnesium powder (**highly flammable**)

Calcium, granules or turnings (**highly flammable**)

Barium metal (**flammable** and **harmful**), cut into small pieces. Use a hacksaw to cut the barium. (The teacher may prefer to demonstrate the reaction of barium with water.)

Magnesium oxide

Calcium hydroxide

Barium hydroxide (**harmful solid**)

Hydrated magnesium chloride

Hydrated calcium chloride

Hydrated barium chloride (**toxic solid**)

Magnesium carbonate

Calcium carbonate

Barium carbonate (**harmful solid**)

Lime water

Approximately 0.1 mol dm⁻³ solutions of:

Mg^{2+} (25 g of $Mg(NO_3)_2.6H_2O$ or 20 g of $MgCl_2.6H_2O$ per dm³)

Ca^{2+} (25 g of $Ca(NO_3)_2.4H_2O$ or 10 g of anhydrous $CaCl_2$ per dm³)

Ba^{2+} (25 g of $Ba(NO_3)_2$ or 25 g of $BaCl_2.2H_2O$ per dm³) (**harmful solution**)

Approximately 1.0 mol dm⁻³ solutions of:

OH^- (40 g of NaOH per dm³) (**corrosive**)

CO_3^{2-} (100 g of anhydrous Na_2CO_3 per dm³)

SO_4^{2-} (300 g of $Na_2SO_4.10H_2O$ per dm³)

250 cm³ of each of these six solutions is enough.

Time required 1–2 hours

Introduction

The *s*-block of the periodic table contains the most reactive and, in chemical terms, the most typically metallic elements. All the elements in Group I are highly reactive, but those in Group II are slightly less so and show a rather more obvious trend in reactivity. In this practical you will study some of the properties of the elements of Group II and their compounds. The members of the group are shown in table 1.

The elements of Group II	
Beryllium	Be
Magnesium	Mg
Calcium	Ca
Strontium	Sr
Barium	Ba
Radium	Ra

Table 1

We shall concentrate on the three elements magnesium, calcium and barium. Beryllium will not be studied because its compounds are extremely toxic and very expensive.

Some data concerning the elements of Group II are given in table 2.

1 What type of ion is formed by Group II elements when they react?

2 Why do ionisation energies decrease as you go down Group II?

3 Why do atomic radii increase as you go down Group II?

4 Which of the various sets of data in table 2 gives the most accurate indication of the likely reactivity trend within the group?

Try to use the data in table 2 when interpreting the results of your experimental work.

Element	Be	Mg	Ca	Sr	Ba
Electron structure	$[He]2s^2$	$[Ne]3s^2$	$[Ar]4s^2$	$[Kr]5s^2$	$[Xe]6s^2$
First ionisation energy/kJ mol^{-1}	900	740	590	550	500
Second ionisation energy/kJ mol^{-1}	1800	1450	1150	1060	970
Third ionisation energy/kJ mol^{-1}	14 800	7700	4900	4200	—
Atomic radius (metallic radius)/nm	0.11	0.16	0.20	0.21	0.22
Ionic radius (M^{2+})/nm	0.030	0.065	0.094	0.110	0.134
Hydration energy (M^{2+})/kJ mol^{-1}	—	−1891	−1561	−1414	−1273
Standard electrode potential, $E^{\ominus}$(M^{2+}(aq) | M(s))/V	−1.85	−2.37	−2.87	−2.89	−2.91

Table 2
Some properties of the group II elements

Procedure

**EYE PROTECTION
MUST BE WORN**

HARMFUL OR TOXIC
Barium compounds

HIGHLY FLAMMABLE
Calcium
Magnesium

CARE
Eye protection must be worn throughout this practical. Barium and its compounds are poisonous. Handle with care and wash your hands after the practical.

Experiment 1:
Reaction of the elements with water

Your teacher may prefer to demonstrate the reaction of barium with water.

Put a very small piece of calcium metal into a large beaker of cold water. Observe the reaction and identify the products. Repeat, using a small piece of *clean* magnesium ribbon (clean with emery paper if necessary). Finally, repeat using a small piece of barium metal.

5 Write equations for any reactions which occur.

6 How do the metals differ in the vigour with which they react with water?

7 In all their reactions the Group II metals behave as reducing agents. What is being reduced in the reaction with water?

8 Explain the reactivity trend among the three metals in this experiment, using some of the data in table 2.

9 What other factor, not listed in the table, may affect the relative reactivity of the metals with water?

The reaction of magnesium with water was probably very slow. You can investigate this reaction further by setting up the experiment shown in figure 1. Leave the experiment for half an hour or so, then test the products.

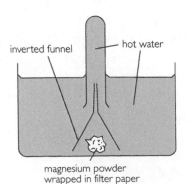

inverted funnel — hot water

magnesium powder
wrapped in filter paper

Figure 1
Investigation of the reaction of magnesium with water.

HARMFUL
Barium hydroxide

**EYE PROTECTION
MUST BE WORN**

Experiment 2:
Acid-base character

Place a very small quantity (about 0.01 g) of magnesium oxide, calcium hydroxide and barium hydroxide in three separate test tubes. Add 10 cm³ of distilled water to each tube, stopper the tube and shake. Add 2 drops of universal indicator solution to each tube and mix. Record the pH values indicated for the three tubes.

10 How does the acid–base character of the hydroxides vary within the group?

11 Write a general ionic equation to represent the equilibrium between the undissolved solid hydroxide, $M(OH)_2(s)$, and its aqueous ions, $M^{2+}(aq)$ and $OH^-(aq)$.

12 Why is it valid to use magnesium oxide instead of magnesium hydroxide in this experiment?

13 What is 'milk of magnesia' and what is it used for?

14 Look at the values for ionic radius in table 2. Which Group II ion will have the strongest attraction for OH^- ions? What effect will this have on the basic strength of its hydroxide?

**EYE PROTECTION
MUST BE WORN**

CORROSIVE
Hydrogen chloride

TOXIC
Hydrogen chloride

HARMFUL
Hydrated barium chloride

**USE A FUME
CUPBOARD**

IRRITANT
Hydrated calcium chloride

Experiment 3:
Hydrolysis of the chlorides

Ionic chlorides dissolve in water forming simple hydrated ions. Many covalent and partly covalent chlorides, however, are hydrolysed, giving hydrogen chloride and the oxide or hydroxide. For example, aluminium chloride reacts vigorously with water as follows:

$$AlCl_3 + 3H_2O \rightarrow Al(OH)_3 + 3HCl$$

The extent of hydrolysis of the Group II chlorides can be estimated by heating the hydrated chloride and testing for hydrogen chloride gas.

Working in a fume cupboard, strongly heat about 1 cm depth of the hydrated chlorides of magnesium, calcium and barium in separate, dry, hard-glass test tubes. Test for the evolution of hydrogen chloride (**CARE toxic**) using damp indicator paper.

15 Are any of the chlorides hydrolysed? Is there a trend in the tendency towards hydrolysis?

16 Which of the chlorides shows the greatest covalent character? Explain this tendency towards covalency in terms of some of the data in table 2.

HARMFUL
Barium carbonate

**EYE PROTECTION
MUST BE WORN**

Experiment 4:
Thermal stability of the carbonates

Strongly heat about 1 cm depth of each of the dry carbonates of magnesium, calcium and barium separately in the apparatus shown in

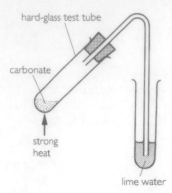

hard-glass test tube

carbonate

strong
heat

lime water

Figure 2
Investigating the thermal stability of
carbonates.

IRRITANT
Solution of hydroxide
ions

**EYE PROTECTION
MUST BE WORN**

HARMFUL
Solution of Ba²⁺ ions

figure 2. Continue heating strongly for several minutes. Note how rapidly gas is evolved, and the extent to which the lime water becomes milky. **Remember to remove the tube from the lime water as soon as heating is stopped, to prevent suck-back.**

> **17** Write equations for any reactions which occur.
>
> **18** What trend do you detect in the thermal stability of the carbonates of the elements of Group II?

Experiment 5:
Solubility of some compounds of Group II elements

To investigate the solubility of Group II compounds, solutions containing the appropriate anions and cations are mixed. If the compound is insoluble, a precipitate will form.

Put 2 cm³ of a 0.1 mol dm⁻³ solution of each of the Group II cations under investigation (Mg^{2+}(aq), Ca^{2+}(aq), Ba^{2+}(aq)) in separate test tubes. Add an equal volume of a 1.0 mol dm⁻³ solution of hydroxide ions, and mix. Remember, do **not** put your thumb over the tube when mixing. Note whether a precipitate is formed, and if so, how dense it is.

Repeat the experiment twice, using first a 1.0 mol dm⁻³ solution of sulphate ions and then a 1.0 mol dm⁻³ solution of carbonate ions, instead of the hydroxide ions. Tabulate your results.

> **19** What trends do you notice in the solubility of:
>
> **a** hydroxides,
> **b** sulphates,
> **c** carbonates?

If you have time, you could extend this experiment by investigating the solubility of some other compounds. You might then be able to formulate a more general rule concerning solubility trends within the group.

> **20** Using the results and conclusions you have derived from this practical, predict the following properties of:
> **a** beryllium, **b** strontium, and their compounds:
>
> **i** reaction with water,
> **ii** acid–base character of the hydroxide,
> **iii** tendency of the chloride to hydrolyse,
> **iv** thermal stability of the carbonate,
> **v** solubility of the hydroxide,
> **vi** solubility of the carbonate,
> **vii** solubility of the sulphate.

Practical 21

The halogens

REQUIREMENTS

Each student will need:

Eye protection

Rack with 4 test tubes

Bunsen burner

Manganese(IV) oxide (**harmful**)

Potassium manganate(VII) (**harmful** and **oxidising**)

Supply of chlorine (**toxic** and **irritant**)

Bromine (very **toxic** and **corrosive**)

Iodine (**harmful**)

Concentrated hydrochloric acid (**corrosive**)

Full-range indicator paper

Chlorine water (**harmful** and **irritant**)

Bromine water (**very toxic** and **corrosive**)

Solution (approximately 1 mol dm^{-3}) of sodium thiosulphate, to be kept near to the bromine water to neutralise any spills

Cyclohexane (**harmful** and **highly flammable**)

Access to fume cupboard

Approximately 1.0 mol dm^{-3} solutions of the following substances:

Iron(II) sulphate (**harmful**)

Sodium hydroxide (**corrosive**)

Potassium chloride

Potassium bromide

Potassium iodide

Time required   1 hour

HARMFUL
Potassium manganate(VII)
Manganese(IV) oxide

CORROSIVE
Concentrated
hydrochloric acid

OXIDISING
Potassium
manganate(VII)

Introduction

In this practical you will compare the properties and reactions of the halogens, a group of reactive non-metals in the periodic table. You will be concentrating on chlorine, bromine and iodine. Fluorine's exceptional reactivity makes it difficult to handle in the school or college laboratory.

> **CARE!**
> *Eye protection must be worn at all times in this practical.*

**EYE PROTECTION
MUST BE WORN**

A   Preparing the halogens

All the methods of preparing halogens involve oxidising halide ions.

$$2\,\text{Hal}^- \rightarrow \text{Hal}_2 + 2e^-$$

> **CARE!**
> *Particular care is needed in the following experiments. Use a fume cupboard, and do not use greater quantities than those given.*

**USE A FUME
CUPBOARD**

Action of manganese(IV) oxide or potassium manganate(VII) on concentrated hydrohalic acid (HCl, HBr, HI)

Warm 1 cm^3 of concentrated hydrochloric acid (CARE) with a spatula measure of manganese(IV) oxide.

> **1** Describe what happens and write an equation (or half-equations) for the reaction occurring.

Add a few drops of concentrated hydrochloric acid to half a spatula measure of potassium manganate(VII).

> **CARE!**
> *Make quite sure you are using hydrochloric acid. Other concentrated acids can have dangerous reactions with potassium manganate(VII).*

> **2** Write an equation (or half-equations) for the reaction occurring.
>
> **3** Compare the action of manganese(IV) oxide and potassium manganate(VII) as oxidising agents in these two simple experiments.

4 Write the halide ions F⁻, Cl⁻, Br⁻ and I⁻ in order of their ease of oxidation.

5 Explain the relative ease of oxidation of the halide ions.

B   Physical properties of the halogens

6 Use a data book to make a table comparing the colour, state at room temperature, melting point and boiling point of the halogens fluorine, chlorine, bromine and iodine.

7 What trends do you notice in the physical properties of the halogens as their relative atomic mass increases?

C   Chemical properties of the halogens

Experiment 1:
Reactions of halogens with water

Working in a fume cupboard, pass chlorine through 5 cm³ of water for a few seconds. Test the pH of the resulting solution with full-range indicator paper.

8 What conclusion can you draw concerning chlorine water from this test?

9 Chlorine water contains dissolved chlorine, together with a mixture of two acids which are formed when chlorine reacts with water. What are these two acids called? Write an equation for the reaction of chlorine with water.

**USE A FUME
CUPBOARD**

**EYE PROTECTION
MUST BE WORN**

TOXIC
Chlorine

**USE A FUME
CUPBOARD**

**WEAR PROTECTIVE
GLOVES**

VERY TOXIC
Bromine

CORROSIVE
Bromine

HARMFUL
Iodine

CARE!
Keep the bromine bottle in a fume cupboard and avoid skin contact by wearing protective gloves. If any bromine is spilt, neutralise it immediately with a solution of sodium thiosulphate(VI). Be careful when adding drops of bromine: it is very dense and some droppers do not hold it well.

Shake **one drop** of bromine with 5 cm³ of water in a test tube until the bromine dissolves. Test the resulting solution with full-range indicator paper.

Repeat the experiment using a small crystal of iodine in place of the bromine.

10 Compare the ease with which the three halogens dissolve in water, the pH of their resulting solutions and their action as bleaching agents.

11 What specific uses does chlorine have as a bleach?

IRRITANT
Chlorine water
Bromine water

**EYE PROTECTION
MUST BE WORN**

VERY TOXIC
Bromine water

CORROSIVE
Bromine water

HARMFUL
Iodine

**USE A FUME
CUPBOARD**

**EYE PROTECTION
MUST BE WORN**

HARMFUL
Iron(II) sulphate

CORROSIVE
Sodium hydroxide
solution

Experiment 2:
Solubility of the halogens in cyclohexane

Shake 3 cm^3 of chlorine water, Cl_2(aq), with 1 cm^3 of cyclohexane in a test tube.

Repeat the experiment using: **a** 3 cm^3 of bromine water, **b** a small crystal of iodine, in place of the 3 cm^3 of chlorine water.

12 Tabulate and explain your observations in the three simple experiments.

Experiment 3:
Halogens as oxidising agents

CARE!
Experiment 3 must be carried out in a fume cupboard.

(1) Reactions with iron(II) sulphate solution

Put 3 cm^3 of iron(II) sulphate solution into each of two test tubes. To one test tube add 3 cm^3 of Cl_2(aq) and to the other add 3 cm^3 of water. This second test tube acts as a control.

13 What is a 'control'?

14 What do you observe in:
   a the first tube,
   b the control tube?

Investigate whether Fe^{2+} ions have been oxidised to Fe^{3+} by adding 1 cm^3 of sodium hydroxide solution to each tube.

15 How does the addition of sodium hydroxide show whether Fe^{2+} ions have been oxidised by chlorine?

16 Write an equation for the reaction of chlorine with iron(II) sulphate.

Repeat the experiment using Br_2(aq) in place of Cl_2(aq).

17 Describe and explain the reaction of Br_2(aq).

(2) The relative reactivity of the halogens as oxidising agents

You can investigate the relative reactivity of the halogens by adding a halogen to solutions of halides.

Investigate the action of Cl_2(aq) on:

   a KBr(aq),
   b KI(aq),

and then the action of $Br_2(aq)$ on:

a KCl(aq),
b KI(aq).

Use 3 cm^3 of each reacting solution. After mixing the aqueous solutions, shake each of the four resulting solutions with 1 cm^3 of cyclohexane.

18 Tabulate the results of the four tests showing the solutions mixed, the changes which occur before cyclohexane is added, and the final colour of the cyclohexane layer.

19 Write equations for the reactions where appropriate.

20 What is the order of oxidising power of the halogens?

21 Look up the electrode potentials of the halogens for the Hal_2/Hal^- systems. Do these confirm your deductions about their relative oxidising power?

Investigation

See Investigation L3

Practical 22

The oxidation states of vanadium and manganese

REQUIREMENTS

Each student, or pair of students, will need:

Eye protection

2 boiling tubes with bung

Rack with 4 test tubes

Filter paper and funnel

Small beaker

Ammonium vanadate(V) (ammonium metavanadate) (NH_4VO_3) (**toxic**)

Manganese(IV) oxide (MnO_2) (**harmful**)

Hydrated manganese(II) sulphate (**harmful**)

2 mol dm^{-3} NaOH (dilute NaOH) (**corrosive**)

1.0 mol dm^{-3} H_2SO_4 (dilute H_2SO_4) (**irritant**)

Granulated zinc

Concentrated HNO_3 (**corrosive**)

Concentrated H_2SO_4 (**corrosive**)

0.01 mol dm^{-3} $KMnO_4$

0.1 mol dm^{-3} $KMnO_4$

Time required

Part A: $\frac{1}{2}$ hour

Part B: $\frac{3}{4}$ hour

Introduction

The atoms of transition metals have electrons of similar energy in both the $3d$ and the $4s$ levels. This means that transition metals can form a number of different stable ions by losing, or sharing different numbers of electrons. Thus, all the transition metals in the first series (titanium to copper) have two or more oxidation states in their compounds.

The intention of this experiment is:

(i) to investigate the chemistry of vanadium and manganese,

(ii) to apply a knowledge of electrode potentials to the reactions studied,

(iii) to prepare some vanadium and manganese compounds in their less common oxidation states.

---

1 The electronic structure of vanadium is (Ar) $3d^3 4s^2$. Write the electronic structures of V^+, V^{2+} and V^{3+}. (Remember that electrons will be lost from the $4s$ sub-shell before the $3d$ sub-shell.)

2 Which of these ions has the most stable electronic structure? Explain your answer.

3 Vanadium(III) compounds are much more common than vanadium(II) and vanadium(I) compounds. What factors might be responsible for this?

EYE PROTECTION MUST BE WORN

CARE!
Eye protection must be worn throughout this practical.

A   Oxidation states of vanadium

Step-by-step conversion of vanadium(V) to vanadium(II)

CARE!
Vanadium compounds are toxic.

Dissolve 1 g of ammonium vanadate(V) (NH_4VO_3) in 10 cm^3 of 2 mol dm^{-3} sodium hydroxide solution in a boiling tube. Then add 20 cm^3 of 1.0 mol dm^{-3} sulphuric acid. This solution contains dioxovanadium(V) ions, VO_2^+, in acid solution.

$$VO_3^-(aq) + 2H^+(aq) \rightarrow VO_2^+(aq) + H_2O(l)$$

IRRITANT
Dilute sulphuric acid

CORROSIVE
Sodium hydroxide solution

TOXIC
Vanadium compounds

Now add a few pieces of granulated zinc to the mixture. Close the boiling tube with a rubber bung and shake steadily until no further changes occur. Remove the bung to release pressure from time to time.

> 4 Describe what happens as the tube is shaken.
>
> 5 Copy and complete table 1, recording the colours of the various oxidation states to which vanadium is successively reduced. (**Note**: the first green colour which you see is a mixture of the original vanadium(V) solution and vanadium (IV)).

Ion	VO_2^+	VO^{2+}	V^{3+}	V^{2+}
Name	dioxovanadium(V) ion	oxovanadium(IV) ion	vanadium(III) ion	vanadium(II) ion
Oxidation state				
Colour				

Table 1
Oxidation states of vanadium

The standard electrode potentials for the reactions involved are:

$$VO_2^+ + 2H^+ + e^- \rightarrow VO^{2+} + H_2O \qquad E^\ominus = +1.00 \text{ V}$$
$$VO^{2+} + 2H^+ + e^- \rightarrow V^{3+} + H_2O \qquad E^\ominus = +0.32 \text{ V}$$
$$V^{3+} + e^- \rightarrow V^{2+} \qquad E^\ominus = -0.26 \text{ V}$$
$$Zn^{2+} + 2e^- \rightarrow Zn \qquad E^\ominus = -0.76 \text{ V}$$

> 6 Explain why zinc is capable of reducing VO_2^+ to V^{2+}.
>
> 7 Which of the stages in the reduction of vanadium(V) to vanadium(II) would you expect to be achieved least readily? Explain your answer.

CORROSIVE
Concentrated nitric acid

EYE PROTECTION MUST BE WORN

When no further colour changes occur, filter the mixture to obtain 5 cm³ of the final solution. Now add concentrated nitric acid drop by drop to the 5 cm³ of filtrate, shaking very carefully.

> 8 Describe what happens. To which oxidation state does nitric acid oxidise vanadium(II)?
>
> 9 Do your results agree with the standard electrode potentials above and that for nitric acid below? Explain.

$$NO_3^- + 2H^+ + e^- \rightarrow NO_2 + H_2O \qquad E^\ominus = +0.80 \text{ V}$$

B   Oxidation states of manganese

HARMFUL
Manganese compounds

You may have used the following compounds of manganese already: potassium manganate(VII), $KMnO_4$ (also called potassium permanganate), manganese(IV) oxide, MnO_2, and manganese(II) sulphate, $MnSO_4$.

10 Prepare an oxidation number chart for manganese and write MnO_4^-, MnO_2, Mn^{2+} and Mn on the appropriate lines of the chart.

The commonest oxidation states of manganese are +7, +4 and +2. In the next experiment, we shall investigate the preparation of manganese(VI) and manganese(III) compounds.

The preparation of manganese(VI) compounds

11 Use the following electrode potentials to explain why Mn(VI) cannot be prepared by reacting Mn(VII) with Mn(IV) in *acid* solution.

In acid:

$$MnO_4^- + e^- \rightarrow MnO_4^{2-} \qquad\qquad E^\ominus = +0.56 \text{ V}$$
$$Mn(VII) \qquad Mn(VI)$$
$$4H^+ + MnO_4^{2-} + 2e^- \rightarrow MnO_2 + 2H_2O \qquad E^\ominus = +2.26 \text{ V}$$
$$Mn(VI) \qquad\qquad Mn(IV)$$

12 Would increasing the concentration of either MnO_4^- or H^+ improve the chances of preparing Mn(VI)? Explain.

13 Why is the reaction more likely to yield Mn(VI) in *alkaline* solution?

14 Do the following electrode potentials suggest that Mn(VI) *might* be prepared from Mn(VII) and Mn(IV) in *alkaline* solution? Explain.

In alkali:

$$MnO_4^- + e^- \rightarrow MnO_4^{2-} \qquad\qquad E^\ominus = +0.56 \text{ V}$$
$$2H_2O + MnO_4^{2-} + 2e^- \rightarrow MnO_2 + 4OH^- \qquad E^\ominus = +0.59 \text{ V}$$

15 Increasing the concentration of either MnO_4^- or OH^- will improve the chance of preparing Mn(VI). Why is this?

You can now test these predictions. Put 10 cm^3 portions of 0.01 mol dm^{-3} $KMnO_4$ into each of two boiling tubes. Add 5 cm^3 of dilute sulphuric acid to one tube and 5 cm^3 of dilute sodium hydroxide solution to the other. Now add a little manganese(IV) oxide to each tube and shake for two minutes. Filter each mixture into a clean test tube.

16 In which tube has a reaction occurred? (The colour of Mn(VI) is green.)

To the green solution add 5 cm^3 of dilute sulphuric acid.

17 Describe and explain what happens.

18 Use the following electrode potentials to predict whether Mn(III) could be prepared by reacting Mn(II) and Mn(IV) in *acid* solution. Explain your answer.

In acid:

$$4H^+ + MnO_2 + e^- \rightarrow Mn^{3+} + 2H_2O \qquad E^\ominus = +0.95 \text{ V}$$
$$Mn^{3+} + e^- \rightarrow Mn^{2+} \qquad E^\ominus = +1.51 \text{ V}$$

19 Use the following electrode potentials to predict whether Mn(III) could be prepared by reacting Mn(II) and Mn(IV) in *alkaline* solution.

In alkali:

$$2H_2O + MnO_2 + e^- \rightarrow Mn(OH)_3 + OH^- \qquad E^\ominus = +1.51 \text{ V}$$
$$Mn(OH)_3 + e^- \rightarrow Mn(OH)_2 \qquad E^\ominus = -0.10 \text{ V}$$

20 Write an overall equation for the reaction in alkaline solution. Include state symbols.

21 Why is the rate of this reaction very slow?

Another possible way of obtaining Mn(III) might be to react Mn(II) with Mn(VII).

In acid:

$$8H^+ + MnO_4^- + 5e^- \rightarrow Mn^{2+} + 4H_2O \qquad E^\ominus = +1.51 \text{ V}$$
$$Mn^{3+} + e^- \rightarrow Mn^{2+} \qquad E^\ominus = +1.51 \text{ V}$$

22 Do these electrode potentials suggest that Mn^{3+} *might* be obtained by reacting MnO_4^- with Mn^{2+}? Explain.

23 Would increasing the concentration of acid improve the chance of preparing Mn(III)?

Procedure

Dissolve 0.5 g of hydrated manganese(II) sulphate in about 2 cm^3 of dilute sulphuric acid and add 10 drops of concentrated sulphuric acid. Cool the test tube in cold water and then add 5 drops of 0.1 mol dm^{-3} potassium manganate(VII).

CORROSIVE
Concentrated sulphuric acid

EYE PROTECTION MUST BE WORN

24 Describe what happens. What is the colour of aqueous Mn^{3+} ions?

Pour the final solution into 50 cm^3 of water.

25 Describe and explain what happens.

Practical 23

Copper and copper compounds

REQUIREMENTS

Each student, or pair of students, will need:

Eye protection

Rack and 6 test tubes

2 boiling tubes

2 hard-glass ignition tubes

Beaker (100 cm^3)

Beaker (250 cm^3)

Filter funnel

Filter paper

Dropping pipette

Copper foil

Copper turnings

Potassium sodium 2,3-dihydroxybutanedioate (tartrate) (Rochelle salt)

Glucose

Copper(II) oxide (**harmful**)

Copper(II) chloride (anhydrous) (**toxic**)

Copper(II) bromide (anhydrous) (**toxic**)

Dilute hydrochloric acid (2 mol dm^{-3}) (**irritant**)

Dilute sulphuric acid (1 mol dm^{-3}) (**irritant**)

Dilute nitric acid (2 mol dm^{-3}) (**corrosive**)

Concentrated hydrochloric acid (**corrosive**)

Dilute sodium hydroxide solution (2 mol dm^{-3}) (**corrosive**)

Dilute ammonia (2 mol dm^{-3})

Solutions, about 0.25 mol dm^{-3}, of:

- copper(II) sulphate
- potassium iodide
- sodium thiosulphate

Access to fume cupboard

Time required 2 hours

Introduction

The intention of this practical is to:

(i) revise some of the basic reactions of copper and copper compounds,
(ii) compare copper(I) and copper(II) compounds.

A   Basic reactions of copper and copper compounds

> **CARE!**
> *Eye protection must be worn throughout this practical.*

EYE PROTECTION MUST BE WORN

CORROSIVE
Sodium hydroxide solution
Dilute nitric acid

a Hold a piece of clean copper foil with tongs. Heat it in a roaring bunsen flame.

b Drop one copper turning into 2 cm^3 of dilute nitric acid and warm. Identify the gas evolved.

c Add dilute sodium hydroxide solution drop by drop to 2 cm^3 of copper(II) sulphate solution, until the sodium hydroxide is in excess.

d Add ammonia solution drop by drop to 2 cm^3 of copper(II) sulphate solution until the ammonia is in excess.

1 For each of the reactions **a** to **c**, decide what has been formed and write an equation.

2 Reaction **d** finally results in the formation of a complex ion containing Cu^{2+} and ammonia.

$$Cu(H_2O)_4^{2+}(aq) + 4NH_3(aq) \rightleftharpoons Cu(NH_3)_4^{2+}(aq) + 4H_2O(l)$$
pale blue   deep blue

Explain your observations in reaction **d** in terms of this equilibrium.

3 What is the oxidation state of copper in all the compounds formed in these introductory experiments?

4 What other oxidation states does copper have besides this one?

5 The atomic number of copper is 29. Its 29 electrons are arranged in sub-shells as:

$1s^2 2s^2 2p^6 3s^2 3p^6 3d^{10} 4s^1$

How many electrons would you expect a copper atom to lose in forming its compounds, in view of the tendency of atoms to achieve stable electron structures?

6 Does it surprise you that the commonly encountered oxidation state of copper is 2+? Explain.

7 Given the electron structure of the Cu^+ ion, what colour would you expect copper(I) compounds to be?

The electronic structure of copper suggests that its stable oxidation state should be 1+. But experience shows that the 2+ state is more stable under normal conditions. However, Cu(I) compounds do exist, and in the second part of this practical you will prepare some of them. Your results should help you to understand why, under normal conditions, Cu(II) is more common than Cu(I).

B Copper(I) and copper(II) compounds

CARE!
Eye protection must be worn.

CORROSIVE
Sodium hydroxide solution

EYE PROTECTION MUST BE WORN

Experiment 1:
The preparation of copper(I) oxide

Copper(I) oxide is normally made by reducing Cu^{2+} ions in alkaline solution. This reaction forms the basis of Fehling's and Benedict's tests for reducing sugars.

Put about 5 cm^3 of copper(II) sulphate solution in a boiling tube. In a separate boiling tube mix 5 cm^3 of sodium hydroxide solution and about 1 g of potassium sodium tartrate (Rochelle salt). Add this solution to the copper(II) sulphate until the precipitate formed at first just dissolves. You now have Fehling's solution. (This contains a complex ion containing Cu^{2+} and tartrate ions in an alkaline solution.)

Now add about 1 g of glucose to the mixture and boil carefully until an orange-red precipitate forms.

Allow the precipitate to settle (centrifuge if necessary). Then decant the solution and wash the precipitate with distilled water. Keep the precipitate for use in experiment **2**.

The orange-red precipitate is copper(I) oxide.

8 What substance acted as the reducing agent in converting Cu(II) to Cu(I)?

9 What is the purpose of the tartrate ions in this experiment?

10 Cu^+ ions do not form a complex with tartrate. Instead, they react with OH^- in the alkaline solution to form copper(I) hydroxide. This decomposes to copper(I) oxide when the mixture is boiled. Write equations for these two reactions.

IRRITANT
Dilute sulphuric acid
Dilute hydrochloric
acid

**EYE PROTECTION
MUST BE WORN**

HARMFUL
Copper(I) oxide

CORROSIVE
Dilute nitric acid

Experiment 2:
The reactions of copper(I) oxide and copper(II) oxide with acids

Put a small quantity (about 0.1 g) of your copper(I) oxide in each of three test tubes. Put a similar amount of copper(II) oxide in each of three further tubes. Use the tubes to investigate the reaction of each oxide with dilute hydrochloric acid, dilute sulphuric acid and dilute nitric acid in turn. Add the acid slowly to the oxide until acid is present in excess, then warm gently and observe **carefully** to see what is formed. (In some cases there is more than one product.)

11 Tabulate your observations.

12 Does copper(I) oxide react with dilute sulphuric acid to form Cu^+ or Cu^{2+} ions?

13 What other product is formed in the reaction of copper(I) oxide with dilute sulphuric acid?

14 What happens to the Cu^+ ion when copper(I) oxide reacts with dilute sulphuric acid?

15 Is the reaction with dilute nitric acid similar? If not, why not?

16 What is the oxidation state of copper in the product from the reaction of copper(I) oxide with dilute hydrochloric acid?

17 Your results in experiment **2** should show that copper(I) can exist under certain conditions but under other conditions the Cu^+ ion disproportionates. What is meant by disproportionation?

18 To what does Cu^+ disproportionate in the reaction of copper(I) oxide with dilute sulphuric acid?

Experiment 3:
The preparation of copper(I) chloride

The Cu^+ ion normally disproportionates in aqueous solution, but it is quite stable under non-aqueous conditions. Copper(I) chloride is insoluble, so it is not subject to the disproportionation that Cu^+ undergoes in aqueous solution. Copper(I) also forms a complex ion, $CuCl_2^-$, in the presence of excess chloride ions, and this increases the stability of copper(I) chloride relative to copper(II) chloride. This means that copper(I) chloride is quite stable and easily prepared. In fact, it can be prepared by reversing the normal disproportionation of copper(I) and reacting copper(II) with copper metal.

Put about 0.5 g of copper(II) oxide in a boiling tube and add 5–10 cm^3 of concentrated hydrochloric acid. Warm this mixture in a fume cupboard to obtain a clear green solution of copper(II) chloride. Now add about 1 g of copper turnings and boil gently for five minutes.

Filter the resulting solution into about 200 cm^3 of distilled water in a beaker. Allow the precipitate of copper(I) chloride to settle, then decant off the water.

CARE!
Eye protection must be worn.

HARMFUL
Copper(I) chloride

**EYE PROTECTION
MUST BE WORN**

19 Write an equation for the formation of copper(I) chloride from copper metal and copper(II) chloride.

20 Is copper(I) chloride a typical transition metal compound? Compare your answer with the answer you gave to question 7.

21 What similarities are there between copper(I) chloride and silver chloride, AgCl? Why would you expect copper(I) chloride to resemble silver chloride?

22 Bearing in mind the similarity of copper(I) chloride and silver chloride, predict the effect of ammonia solution on solid copper(I) chloride.

Test your prediction by adding 5 cm^3 of ammonia solution to a little solid copper(I) chloride in a test tube.

23 Record your results and try to explain what has happened.

Although copper(I) chloride is insoluble in water, it forms a soluble complex ion with excess chloride ions:

$$CuCl(s) + Cl^-(aq) \rightleftharpoons CuCl_2^-(aq)$$

CORROSIVE
Concentrated hydrochloric acid

Add 2 cm^3 of concentrated hydrochloric acid (**CARE**) to a small amount of your copper(I) chloride in a test tube. Note what happens, then pour the contents of the tube into about 50 cm^3 of cold water in a small beaker.

24 Record your observations and explain them in terms of the equilibrium between CuCl and CuCl$_2^-$.

25 Re-examine the copper(I) chloride. Are there any signs of reversion to the copper(II) state?

TOXIC
Anhydrous copper(II) bromide

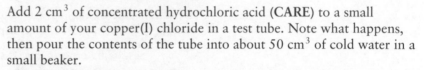

USE A FUME CUPBOARD

TOXIC
Anhydrous copper(II) chloride

Experiment 4:
The thermal decomposition of copper(II) halides

The previous experiments show that copper(I) chloride is fairly stable with respect to copper(II) chloride. Perhaps copper(II) chloride will decompose to copper(I) chloride when it is heated.

Working in a fume cupboard, heat very small samples of anhydrous copper(II) chloride and anhydrous copper(II) bromide in separate hard-glass ignition tubes. Heat gently at first, then more strongly. Observe closely to see if any gases are evolved, and note the appearance of the residues.

26 Do the halides decompose on heating? Write equations for any reactions that occur.

27 Which halide decomposed more readily?

28 How stable would you expect copper(II) iodide to be relative to copper(I) iodide?

Experiment 5:
The preparation of copper(I) iodide

Add 3 cm^3 of potassium iodide solution to 3 cm^3 of copper(II) sulphate solution in a test tube. Note carefully what happens, and allow the contents of the tube to settle. Add sodium thiosulphate solution to the tube until the solution is clear and you can tell the colour of the solid that has been formed.

29 What substances are produced when KI reacts with $CuSO_4$?
    Write an equation for the reaction.

30 Does the result of this reaction agree with your answer to
    question 28?

31 In this practical you have prepared copper in both oxidation
    states, + 1 and + 2. Summarise the conditions which favour the
    existence of each of the two oxidation states.

32 Is copper a transition metal?

See
Investigation L5

Practical 24

Identifying cations

REQUIREMENTS

Each student will need:

Eye protection

Concentrated hydrochloric acid (**corrosive**)

The following solids for flame tests: barium chloride (**toxic**), calcium chloride (**irritant**), copper chloride (**toxic**), magnesium chloride, potassium chloride, sodium chloride, ammonium chloride (**harmful**)

Aqueous solutions (approx. 0.1 mol dm^{-3}) of the following cations:

Al^{3+}, Ag^+, Ca^{2+}, Cr^{3+}, Cu^{2+}, Fe^{2+}, Fe^{3+}, K^+, Mg^{2+}, Mn^{2+}, Na^+, NH_4^+, Ni^{2+}, Pb^{2+}(**toxic**), Sn^{2+}, Zn^{2+}

Sodium hydroxide solution (approximately 2.0 mol dm^{-3}) (**corrosive**)

Dilute nitric acid (approx. 2.0 mol dm^{-3}) (**corrosive**)

Unknown soluble solids containing a single cation and labelled X, Y, etc.

Nichrome wire

Bunsen burner

Watch glass

Rack with 4 test tubes

Filter funnel

Filter paper

Time required   2 hours

Introduction

Many common cations can be identified from the colour of their hydroxides or the colour they produce during flame tests.

The intention of this practical is to develop a simple, systematic method of identifying the following cations, provided there is only one cation present in the substance under test:

Al^{3+}, Ag^+, Ba^{2+}, Ca^{2+}, Cr^{3+}, Cu^{2+}, Fe^{2+}, Fe^{3+}, K^+, Mg^{2+}, Mn^{2+}, Na^+, NH_4^+, Ni^{2+}, Pb^{2+}, Sn^{2+}, Zn^{2+}.

EYE PROTECTION MUST BE WORN

> **CARE!**
> *Eye protection must be worn throughout this practical.*

Appearance

The colour of a substance may give a clue to its identity and the cation it contains, as shown in table 1 below.

Colour	Inference
White or colourless	Probably does not contain a transition metal cation
Not white or transparent	Probably contains a transition metal cation
Blue	Possibly contains Cu^{2+} or Ni^{2+}
Green	Possibly contains Cu^{2+}, Cr^{3+}, Fe^{2+} or Ni^{2+}
Yellow or brown	Possibly contains Fe^{3+}

Table 1
The colours of substances and their constituent cations

Preparing a solution of the substance

CORROSIVE
Concentrated hydrochloric acid
Dilute nitric acid

EYE PROTECTION MUST BE WORN

If you are provided with a solid, it is most convenient to carry out a flame test on this. After the flame test, you will need to make an aqueous solution of the substance before other tests are carried out.

Put one spatula-full of the substance (i.e. 0.2 g–0.4 g) in a test tube and shake this with about 5 cm^3 of distilled water. If the solid will not dissolve in cold water, warm gently.

If the solid is insoluble in water, try cold and then hot dilute nitric acid. If this fails, consult your teacher. It may be necessary to use concentrated hydrochloric acid.

Flame tests

CARE!
Eye protection must be worn for flame tests.

IRRITANT
Calcium chloride

TOXIC
Copper chloride
Barium chloride

Dip a nichrome wire in concentrated hydrochloric acid. Then heat it in a roaring bunsen flame until it no longer gives colour to the flame. The wire is now clean. Mix a little barium chloride with concentrated hydrochloric acid on a watch glass, moisten the wire with this solution and hold the wire in the bunsen flame. Clean the wire thoroughly again and repeat the test with the chlorides of Ca^{2+}, Cu^{2+}, Mg^{2+}, K^+ and Na^+ in turn.

1 What are the flame colours (if any) of the following metal ions?
   a Ba^{2+} b Ca^{2+} c Cu^{2+} d Mg^{2+} e K^+ f Na^+

2 Why do certain metal ions give flame colours in this way?

3 One of the six metal ions tested gives no flame colour. Why is this?

CORROSIVE
Sodium hydroxide
solution

**EYE PROTECTION
MUST BE WORN**

TOXIC
Solutions of lead(II) compounds
Solutions of barium compounds

Testing with sodium hydroxide solution

Add a few drops of sodium hydroxide solution to 3 cm^3 of a solution containing $Al^{3+}(aq)$.

4 What happens? Write an equation for the reaction.

5 Does the precipitate remain or dissolve when *excess* $NaOH(aq)$ is added?

Repeat the experiment with solutions containing the following cations in place of Al^{3+}:

Ag^+, Ba^{2+}, Ca^{2+}, Cr^{3+}, Cu^{2+}, Fe^{2+}, Fe^{3+}, K^+, Mg^{2+}, Mn^{2+}, Na^+, NH_4^+, Ni^{2+}, Pb^{2+}, Sn^{2+}, Zn^{2+}.

Record your results in a table similar to table 2.

Cation tested	What happens when a few drops of NaOH(aq) are added to 3 cm^3 of the cation solution?	What happens when excess NaOH(aq) is added?
Al^{3+}	White precipitate of $Al(OH)_3$ forms. $Al^{3+}(aq) + 3OH^-(aq) \rightarrow Al(OH)_3(s)$	White precipitate dissolves forming a clear solution $Al(OH)_3(s) + OH^-(aq) \rightarrow Al(OH)_4^-(aq)$

Table 2
Reactions of cations with sodium hydroxide solution

(The table has been completed for Al^{3+} to show you what is required.) Write the colours and formulae of precipitates, write equations for reactions and say whether precipitates remain or dissolve when excess sodium hydroxide is added.

6 Which cations give no precipitate with NaOH(aq)?

7 How can these three cations be distinguished using flame tests?

8 Which cations give a white precipitate with NaOH(aq) which remains with excess NaOH(aq)?

9 How can these two cations be distinguished using flame tests?

10 Which cations give distinctive coloured precipitates with NaOH(aq)?

Al^{3+}, Pb^{2+}, Sn^{2+} and Zn^{2+} give white precipitates with NaOH(aq) which dissolve in excess. These four ions cannot be distinguished by flame tests.

Precipitate further samples of $Al(OH)_3$, $Pb(OH)_2$, $Sn(OH)_2$ and $Zn(OH)_2$. Filter each precipitate and heat a sample of it to dryness. Copy out and complete table 3.

Precipitate	Colour before heating	What happens on heating	Colour after heating
$Al(OH)_3$			
$Pb(OH)_2$			
$Sn(OH)_2$			
$Zn(OH)_2$			

Table 3

11 How can Al^{3+}, Pb^{2+}, Sn^{2+} and Zn^{2+} be distinguished?

Identifying the cation in an unknown substance

Use the information you have gathered in the previous tests to identify the cation in each of the unknown substances provided by your teacher.

Further work

If time permits, develop a table similar to the one that you have obtained for the reactions of cations with NaOH, showing their reactions with ammonia solution.

Investigation
See
Investigation L5

Practical 25

Alkanes

REQUIREMENTS

Each student, or pair of students, will need:

Eye protection

Rack and 4 test tubes

Boiling tube

Beaker (250 cm^3)

Small glass trough or large beaker

Hard-glass watch glass

Boiling tubes fitted with bungs and glass bends as in figure 1

Aluminium foil

Glass wool

Splints

Access to a bright light source (ideally sunlight, but a high intensity lamp or even a fluorescent light tube will do)

Hexane or cyclohexane (**harmful** and **highly flammable**)

Paraffin oil (medicinal paraffin)

Paraffin wax

Bromine (**very toxic** and **corrosive**). Sodium thiosulphate(VI) solution (approximately 1 mol dm^{-3}) should also be available for dealing with bromine spills

Concentrated sulphuric acid (**very corrosive**)

Bromine water (**very toxic** and **corrosive**)

Potassium manganate(VII) (potassium permanganate) solution, about 0.1 mol dm^{-3}

Dilute sodium hydroxide solution (**corrosive**)

Access to a fume cupboard

Time required   1–2 hours

Introduction

The alkanes are the simplest family of hydrocarbons. They often form the basic skeletons to which functional groups are attached in more complex organic compounds. They are in many ways the most important homologous series, because they are the main constituents of crude oil, from which most organic chemical products are derived.

In this practical you will investigate some of the physical and chemical properties of alkanes. You will be working with a number of different alkanes or mixtures of alkanes.

Methane, CH$_4$	Natural gas from the laboratory gas taps is a good source. (North Sea gas is about 95% methane, most of the remainder being higher alkanes.)
Hexane, C$_6$H$_{14}$	Cyclohexane is a good substitute if hexane is not available. Cycloalkanes have very similar properties to straight-chain alkanes.
Medicinal paraffin	A liquid mixture of long-chain alkanes.
Paraffin wax	A solid mixture of long-chain alkanes.

> **CARE!**
> *Eye protection must be worn throughout this practical.*

EYE PROTECTION MUST BE WORN

Physical properties

Volatility

Use a data book to answer the following questions.

> 1   What are the boiling points of methane and hexane?
>
> 2   Which is the first straight-chain alkane to be liquid at room temperature and pressure?
>
> 3   Which alcohol has a boiling point closest to that of hexane? Comment on your answer.

Solubility

Put 2 cm^3 to 3 cm^3 of hexane in a test tube and add about twice this volume of water. Shake, then stand the tube in a rack.

HIGHLY FLAMMABLE
Hexane
Cyclohexane

HARMFUL
Hexane
Cyclohexane

4 Does hexane dissolve in water? Suggest a reason why the two liquids behave in this way.

5 Is hexane more or less dense than water?

6 Use a data book to discover how the densities of straight-chain alkanes change as their relative molecular masses increase.

Chemical properties

Action of some common reagents on hexane

VERY CORROSIVE
Concentrated
sulphuric acid
Sodium hydroxide
solution

**EYE PROTECTION
MUST BE WORN**

VERY TOXIC
Bromine water

CORROSIVE
Bromine water

Use about 2 cm^3 of hexane and 2 cm^3 of the reagent in each case, shake carefully and look for any signs of a chemical reaction having occurred.

Investigate the reaction of hexane (a typical alkane) with:

a bromine water,

b potassium manganate(VII) solution,

c sodium hydroxide solution,

d concentrated sulphuric acid (**CARE**).

7 Does hexane react with any of the above substances under normal laboratory conditions?

8 The alkanes used to be called the **paraffins**. Suggest why this name was used.

9 In which substance is bromine more soluble – hexane or water? Why?

10 In which substance is potassium manganate(VII) more soluble – hexane or water? Why?

The experiments you have carried out suggest that with common reagents under ordinary laboratory conditions, alkanes are very unreactive. Alkanes are not, however, completely inert. If they were they would not be very useful to humans.

Reaction of hexane with bromine

In the experiment above, you found that hexane does not react with bromine water. In this experiment you will investigate the reaction of hexane with pure bromine, in the presence of sunlight.

**WEAR PROTECTIVE
GLOVES**

**EYE PROTECTION
MUST BE WORN**

> ### CARE!
> *Bromine is corrosive and very toxic. Wear eye protection and protective gloves and work in a fume cupboard when adding the bromine. If any bromine is spilt, neutralise it immediately with a solution of sodium thiosulphate(VI).*

**USE A FUME
CUPBOARD**

VERY TOXIC
Bromine

CORROSIVE
Bromine

Put 2 cm^3 of hexane in each of two test tubes. Add **one drop** of bromine (not bromine water) to each tube. Be careful when adding drops of bromine: it is very dense and some droppers do not hold it well.

Wrap aluminium foil around one of the tubes so that it is light-proof, then stand the two tubes side by side in a test tube rack. Leave the rack in bright sunlight or near to a bright light source for 5–10 minutes, then examine the appearance of each tube. Look for any signs of a gas being evolved.

> **11** Under what conditions does hexane react with bromine?
>
> **12** What inorganic product is formed in this reaction?
>
> **13** Write a structural formula for one possible organic product of the reaction.
>
> **14** What type of reaction is this?

Combustion of alkanes

EXTREMELY FLAMMABLE
Methane

Fill a boiling tube with methane from the gas tap. Stopper the tube and stand it in a rack. Light a splint, unstopper the tube and apply the lighted splint to the mouth of the tube.

> **15** Write a balanced equation for the reaction which occurs.
>
> **16** Would you expect the same result if you held the tube upside down and lighted the gas? Explain your answer.

Put a small piece of paraffin wax on a hard-glass watch glass and apply a lighted splint to it.

> **17** Can the wax be easily ignited?
>
> **18** Why is wax harder to ignite than methane, even though they both contain alkanes?
>
> **19** Why does a candle have a wick?

Cracking of alkanes

At high temperatures, the atoms in an alkane molecule vibrate rapidly. If the temperature is high enough, the vibration becomes sufficiently vigorous for chemical bonds to break. This breakage of the C–C bonds in alkanes leads to the formation of small hydrocarbon fragments. The process is called **cracking**. The temperature required for cracking can be reduced by the use of solid catalysts.

Set up the apparatus shown in figure 1.

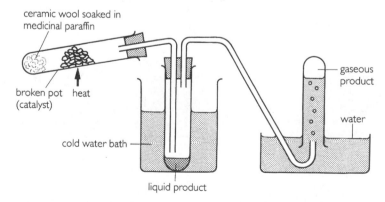

Figure 1
Cracking medicinal paraffin.

**EYE PROTECTION
MUST BE WORN**

CORROSIVE
Bromine water

VERY TOXIC
Bromine water

CARE!
Wear eye protection. When heating the tube, beware of melting the rubber bung, and make sure the delivery tube does not become blocked. Beware of suck-back: remove the delivery tube from the water when you stop heating or when the gas ceases to be evolved.

Heat the broken pot strongly and warm the medicinal paraffin gently so that a steady steam of vapour passes over the hot catalyst. Continue until a few cubic centimetres of liquid product have collected. By this time you should have collected several tubes of gas.

Shake some of the gas with a few drops of bromine water.

20 What happens? What structural feature does the gaseous product's molecule contain?

Test the gaseous product with a burning splint.

Compare the appearance and viscosity of the liquid product with that of the paraffin oil. Shake a little of the liquid product with an equal volume of bromine water in a stoppered tube.

21 What evidence is there that the liquid product contains smaller molecules than the original paraffin oil?

22 Eicosane ($C_{20}H_{42}$) is a typical alkane present in paraffin oil. Write an equation (using structural formulae) to represent one possible outcome of the cracking of eicosane.

23 Why are cracking reactions of this sort important in the petrochemical industry?

24 What would you expect to happen if you repeated the cracking experiment using the liquid product instead of paraffin oil? Test your prediction if you have time.

25 Summarise the important physical and chemical properties of alkanes that you have met in this practical. Where appropriate give an example of the industrial, social or environmental importance of that property.

Practical 26

Alkenes

REQUIREMENTS

Each student, or pair of students, will need;
for the preparation and reactions of ethene:
Eye protection
Ceramic wool
Ethanol (**highly flammable**)
Teat pipette
Bunsen burner
Porous pot
Hard-glass test tube fitted with bung and
delivery tube
4 test tubes with stoppers
Beaker (250 cm^3 or 400 cm^3)
Dilute bromine water (**harmful** and **irritant**)
Dilute potassium manganate(VII) solution
(about 0.1 mol dm^{-3})
Dilute sulphuric acid (**irritant**)
Sodium carbonate solution (about
0.1 mol dm^{-3})

For the preparation and reactions of
cyclohexene:
Eye protection
Round-bottomed or pear-shaped flask
(50 cm^3 or 100 cm^3)
Still-head
Thermometer (0–110 °C) and holder
Liebig condenser
Collecting (receiving) vessel
Beaker (250 cm^3 or 400 cm^3)
Cyclohexanol (**harmful** and **flammable**)
Concentrated phosphoric(V) acid (**corrosive**)
Measuring cylinder (10 cm^3)
Separating funnel
Rack and 3 test tubes with stoppers
Small conical flask
Small crucible
Teat pipette
Saturated sodium chloride solution
Anhydrous calcium chloride (**irritant**)
Ceramic wool
Dilute bromine water (**harmful** and **irritant**)
Dilute potassium manganate(VII) solution
(about 1.0 mol dm^{-3})
Dilute sulphuric acid (**irritant**)
Concentrated sulphuric acid (**very corrosive**)
Cyclohexane (**harmful** and **highly
flammable**)
Time required
Part A Ethene: 1 hour
Part B Cyclohexene: 2 hours

Introduction

In this practical you will prepare a gaseous alkene, ethene, and a liquid alkene, cyclohexene. You will also look at some of their important reactions.

Preparing alkenes

Large quantities of ethene and propene are obtained industrially from cracking reactions. However, the most convenient method of preparing small amounts of any alkene in the laboratory is by the dehydration of the corresponding alcohol. In this practical you will prepare ethene and cyclohexene from ethanol and cyclohexanol respectively.

1 What is meant by the term 'dehydration'?

2 Write equations using structural formulae for the preparation of: **a** ethene and **b** cyclohexene by dehydration of their corresponding alcohols.

3 What is the most commonly used dehydrating agent?
We could use this reagent or concentrated phosphoric(V) acid to dehydrate alcohols, but in preparing ethene from ethanol we shall use catalytic dehydration, with a catalyst such as aluminium oxide, silicon(IV) oxide or porous pot. The reaction is similar to catalytic cracking.

4 Porous pot is made from clay. What elements does it contain?

A   Ethene

Preparing ethene from ethanol

CARE!
*Eye protection must be worn
throughout this practical.*

**EYE PROTECTION
MUST BE WORN**

HIGHLY FLAMMABLE
Ethanol
Ethene

Arrange the apparatus as in figure 1. Heat the porous pot with a small flame. Do **not** heat the ceramic wool directly. **Remember to remove the delivery tube from the water when you are not heating or when bubbles cease.** This will prevent suck-back occurring. Discard the first test tube of gas and then collect three or four stoppered test tubes of ethene.

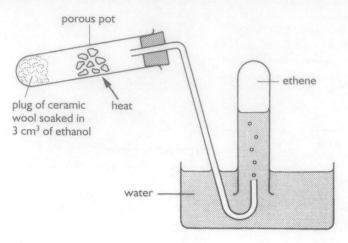

Figure 1
Preparing ethene from ethanol.

5   Why is the ceramic wool not heated directly?

6   Why must the delivery tube be removed from the water when you are not heating?

7   Why should you discard the first test tube of gas?

**EYE PROTECTION
MUST BE WORN**

Reactions of ethene

(1) Burning

Ignite the ethene in one test tube.

8   Describe the flame and write an equation for the combustion.

(2) Reaction with bromine

HARMFUL
Dilute bromine water

IRRITANT
Dilute bromine water
Dilute sulphuric acid

Add 1 cm^3 of dilute bromine water to a test tube of ethene. Stopper the tube and shake.

9   Describe what happens, write an equation for the reaction and name the product.

(3) Reaction with potassium manganate(VII)

Add 1 cm^3 of dilute sulphuric acid and 3 drops of potassium manganate(VII) solution to a test tube of ethene. Stopper the tube and shake.

10   Describe what happens.

The potassium manganate(VII) oxidises ethene to ethane-1,2-diol and other products.

11 What has the KMnO₄ been reduced to?

Repeat this test using 1 cm³ of sodium carbonate solution in place of dilute sulphuric acid.

12 What happens this time?

13 Is the KMnO₄ reduced to the same product as before? Explain your answer.

B   Cyclohexene

Preparing cyclohexene from cyclohexanol

The aims of this experiment are:

A to prepare cyclohexene by dehydrating cyclohexanol using concentrated phosphoric(V) acid,

B to introduce the method for purification of an organic liquid.

14 Concentrated phosphoric(V) acid is preferred to concentrated sulphuric acid as a dehydrating agent for alcohols because it gives a higher yield of alkene? Why does concentrated sulphuric acid give a lower yield of alkene?
(**Hint:** what side reactions occur with concentrated sulphuric acid?)

EYE PROTECTION MUST BE WORN

CORROSIVE
Phosphoric(V) acid

HARMFUL
Cyclohexanol

HIGHLY FLAMMABLE
Cyclohexanol
Cyclohexene

Preparation

Put 10 cm³ of cyclohexanol in a small round-bottomed flask. *Slowly* add 4 cm³ of concentrated phosphoric(V) acid and **mix thoroughly** by swirling the flask cautiously. Now arrange the apparatus as in figure 2.

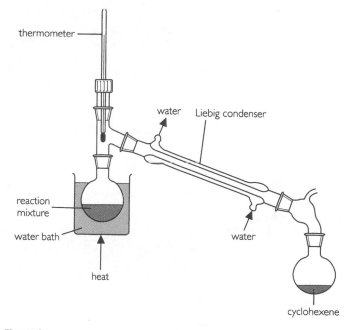

Figure 2
Preparing cyclohexene from cyclohexanol.

Heat the mixture in a water bath at 70 °C for 15 minutes. Raise the temperature and **distil very slowly, so that all the cyclohexene vapour is condensed by the condenser.** Collect the distillate which comes over between 70 °C and 90 °C.

Purification

IRRITANT
Anhydrous calcium chloride

First, wash the distillate to remove impurities. To do this, pour the distillate into a separating funnel and shake it with an equal volume of saturated sodium chloride solution. (Sodium chloride solution is used rather than water because it is denser than water and will separate from the cyclohexene more rapidly after shaking.)

Now you need to dry the cyclohexene. Allow the two layers to separate and then run off the lower aqueous layer. Transfer the top layer (cyclohexene) to a small conical flask and add a few pieces of anhydrous calcium chloride. Mix the contents of the flask until the liquid is clear.

Finally, decant the alkene into a clean round-bottomed flask. Redistil it, collecting the liquid which distils between 81 °C and 85 °C. (The boiling point of cyclohexene is 83 °C.) Weigh the collection flask before and after the distillation, so you can find the mass of cyclohexene obtained. Use your sample of cyclohexene in the experiments below.

15 Name two impurities present in the cyclohexene before purification.

16 What impurities are removed from the impure cyclohexene when it is shaken with sodium chloride solution?

17 Why is the cyclohexene mixed with anhydrous calcium chloride?

18 What are the three key stages in purifying an organic liquid?

19 What mass of cyclohexene did you obtain?

Use the equation for the dehydration of cyclohexanol to calculate the theoretical yield of cyclohexene. (Assume that the phosphoric(V) acid is present in excess.)

20 What is your percentage yield of cyclohexene?

Reactions of cyclohexene

(1) Burning

EYE PROTECTION MUST BE WORN

Burn 1 *drop* of cyclohexene on a small tuft of ceramic wool in a crucible.

21 Suggest four products formed when the cyclohexene burns.

22 Write an equation for the complete combustion of cyclohexene (C_6H_{10}) in excess oxygen.

(2) Reaction with bromine

Add 1 cm^3 of dilute bromine water to 3 drops of cyclohexene in a test tube. Stopper the tube and shake.

HARMFUL
Dillute bromine water

IRRITANT
Dilute bromine water
Dilute sulphuric acid

> **23** Describe what happens, write an equation for the reaction and name the product.

(3) Reaction with potassium manganate(VII)

Add 1 cm^3 of dilute sulphuric acid and 3 drops of potassium manganate(VII) solution to 3 drops of cyclohexene in a test tube. Stopper the tube and shake.

> **24** Describe and explain what happens.

HARMFUL
Cyclohexane

HIGHLY FLAMMABLE
Cyclohexane

VERY CORROSIVE
Concentrated
sulphuric acid

(4) Reaction with concentrated sulphuric acid

Add 3 drops of concentrated sulphuric acid (CARE) to 3 drops of cyclohexene.

> **25** Describe what happens, write an equation and name the product.
>
> **26** Many of the reactions of alkenes involve addition. What do you understand by the term 'addition reaction'?
>
> **27** Why do alkenes readily undergo addition reactions?

Further reactions

If time permits, carry out the reactions again, using cyclohexane in place of cyclohexene.

HARMFUL
Cyclohexane

HIGHLY FLAMMABLE
Cyclohexane

> **28** Account for the differences in reactivity between cyclohexene (a typical alkene) and cyclohexane (a typical alkane).

Practical 27

Aromatic compounds

REQUIREMENTS

Each student, or pair of students, will require:

Part A

Eye protection

Cyclohexane (**highly flammable** and **harmful**)

Cyclohexene (**highly flammable** and **harmful**)

Methylbenzene (**highly flammable** and **harmful**)

Dilute bromine water (**harmful** and **irritant**)

Dilute sulphuric acid (**irritant**)

Dilute potassium manganate(VII) solution (about 0.1 mol dm^{-3})

Rack with 4 test tubes

Part B

Eye protection

Methyl benzoate (**harmful**)

Concentrated sulphuric acid (**very corrosive**)

Concentrated nitric acid (**corrosive** and **oxidising**)

Ice

Ethanol (**highly flammable**)

Conical flask (100 cm^3)

Measuring cylinder (10 cm^3)

Beaker (250 cm^3 or 400 cm^3)

2 small beakers (100 cm^3 or 150 cm^3)

Rack with 2 test tubes

Teat pipette

Thermometer (0 °C–110 °C)

Buchner funnel and flask

Filter paper

Melting point tube

Access to melting point apparatus

Access to suction pump

Access to balance

Time required 2 hours

HIGHLY FLAMMABLE
Cyclohexane
Cyclohexene
Methylbenzene

IRRITANT
Dilute sulphuric acid

Introduction

The simplest and most important aromatic compound is benzene. Indeed, aromatic compounds are normally considered to be those compounds with chemical properties similar to benzene.

1 Write down the full structural formulae of benzene, cyclohexane and methylbenzene.

2 Which of these compounds are:

   a alkanes,   c cyclic compounds,

   b aromatic compounds,   d unsaturated hydrocarbons?

3 What reactions would you expect an unsaturated hydrocarbon to undergo with:
   a bromine water,   b dilute acidified potassium manganate(VII) solution?

Benzene is toxic and cannot be used except in research and industrial production. However, the typical reactions of benzene are also given by methylbenzene, which is safe to use with the right precautions.

A   Addition reactions

In this part of the practical you will compare the properties of methylbenzene, cyclohexane and cyclohexene.

IRRITANT
Dilute bromine water

Reaction with bromine water

Put 1 cm^3 samples of methylbenzene, cyclohexane and cyclohexene into separate test tubes. Add 1 cm^3 of dilute bromine water to each and shake all three mixtures thoroughly.

HARMFUL
Dilute bromine water
Methylbenzene
Cyclohexane
Cyclohexene

HIGHLY FLAMMABLE
Methylbenzene
Cyclohexane
Cyclohexene

4 Make a table of your results. Describe what happens in each case. Write equations where appropriate and name the products of any reactions.

Reaction with acidified potassium manganate(VII)

Put 1 cm^3 samples of methylbenzene, cyclohexane and cyclohexene into separate test tubes. Add 1 cm^3 of dilute sulphuric acid and 1 cm^3 of dilute potassium manganate(VII) solution and shake all three mixtures thoroughly.

5 Make a table of your results. Describe what happens in each case. Write equations where appropriate and name the products of any reactions.

6 Benzene is an unsaturated compound yet it does not react with bromine water or with dilute acidified potassium manganate(VII) solution. Why is this so?

The characteristic reactions of benzene and other aromatic hydrocarbons involve substitution, because this type of reaction retains the delocalised π-electron system of the aromatic nucleus (see *Chemistry in Context*, Fifth Edition, Sections 28.6 and 28.7). Addition reactions involving disruption of the aromatic ring do, however, occur (see *Chemistry in Context*, Fifth Edition, Section 28.8).

7 State the conditions, name the products and write equations for the addition reactions between benzene and

a hydrogen,
b chlorine.

What are the important uses of the products of these two reactions?

B   Substitution reactions

One of the most important substitution reactions of aromatic compounds is nitration. The intention of this experiment is:

1 to illustrate the technique of nitration,
2 to demonstrate the method of purifying an organic solid.

The compound chosen for nitration is methyl benzoate. This is a relatively simple derivative of benzene, of relatively low toxicity, which is used in commercial heat meters. Methyl benzoate can be nitrated readily with a nitric acid/sulphuric acid nitrating mixture. The product is solid methyl 3-nitrobenzoate.

$$O \!=\! C \overset{OCH_3}{\underset{}{}} \text{benzene ring} \quad + HNO_3 \longrightarrow O \!=\! C \overset{OCH_3}{\underset{}{}} \text{benzene ring} \, N \overset{O}{\underset{O}{}} + H_2O$$

(1) Preparation of methyl 3-nitrobenzoate

CARE!
Eye protection must be worn.

Measure 2.5 cm^3 of methyl benzoate into a small conical flask and then dissolve it in 5 cm^3 of concentrated sulphuric acid. When the liquid has dissolved, cool the mixture in ice.

EYE PROTECTION MUST BE WORN

HARMFUL
Methyl benzoate

OXIDISING
Concentrated nitric
acid

CORROSIVE
Concentrated
sulphuric acid
Concentrated nitric
acid

Prepare the nitrating mixture by carefully adding 2 cm³ of concentrated sulphuric acid to 2 cm³ of concentrated nitric acid. Cool this mixture in ice as well.

Now add the nitrating mixture drop by drop from a teat pipette to the solution of methyl benzoate. (Do not allow the nitrating mixture to get into the rubber teat.) Stir the mixture with a thermometer and keep the temperature below 10 °C. When the addition is complete, allow the mixture to stand at room temperature for another 15 minutes.

After this time, pour the reaction mixture on to about 25 g of crushed ice and stir until all the ice has melted and crystalline methyl 3-nitrobenzoate has formed.

(2) Purification of methyl 3-nitrobenzoate

Filter the crystals using a Buchner funnel, wash them thoroughly with cold water and then transfer them to a small beaker.

Now, recrystallise the product from hot ethanol. The idea of recrystallisation is to dissolve the impure product in the minimum possible volume of a hot solvent. When you cool the solution, the product that you want crystallises out of solution, because there is not enough solvent to dissolve it all at the lower temperature. However, the impurities stay behind in solution. Because there is less of these impurities, there is enough solvent to keep them dissolved. You then filter off the crystals of the product from the remaining solution.

Put 15 cm³ of ethanol in a boiling tube. Warm it to about 50 °C by immersing it in a beaker of hot water. The hot water should be obtained using an electric kettle or from a hot water tap. **There should be no naked flames in the laboratory whilst ethanol is being used.** Dissolve all the crystals in the minimum possible volume of this hot ethanol. Allow the solution to cool to room temperature, then immerse the beaker in iced water to complete the crystallisation of methyl 3-nitrobenzoate.

HIGHLY FLAMMABLE
Ethanol

Filter the crystals, dry them between filter papers and then weigh them. Record the mass obtained. Finally, measure the melting point of the crystals. (Pure methyl 3-nitrobenzoate melts at 77.5 °C.)

---

8 One problem with nitration reactions is that further nitration may occur, to give a di- or trinitro-derivative. What conditions used in the preparation helped prevent this?

9 Give the names and structural formulae of two nitro-compounds that are very likely to contaminate the impure crystals of methyl 3-nitrobenzoate.

10 How do the conditions for the nitration of methyl benzoate differ from those for the nitration of benzene?

11 Why were the crystals washed with water before recrystallisation?

12 What happens during a recrystallisation to:
a impurities, **b** the main product?

13 How is loss of the product kept to a minimum during recrystallisation?

14 What are the usual stages in the purification of an organic solid?

15 How many moles of: **a** methyl benzoate, **b** nitric acid, were used in the preparation of methyl 3-nitrobenzoate? (Assume that concentrated nitric acid is pure HNO_3 and that its density is 1.5 g cm^{-3}. Assume that the density of methyl benzoate is 1.1 g cm^{-3}.) Which reactant is present in excess?

16 What is the theoretical yield of methyl 3-nitrobenzoate that should be obtained?

17 What is your actual percentage yield?

Practical 28

1-Bromobutane

REQUIREMENTS

Each student, or pair of students, will need:

Eye protection

Pear-shaped flask (50 cm³)

Round flask (50 cm³)

Condenser

Still-head

Tap funnel to fit still-head (also used as separating funnel)

Thermometer (0 °C–110 °C) and holder

Measuring cylinder (25 cm³)

Teat pipette

Rack with 3 test tubes

Beaker (250 cm³)

Butan-1-ol (**harmful** and **flammable**)

Sodium bromide

Concentrated sulphuric acid (**very corrosive**)

Anhydrous sodium sulphate

Concentrated hydrochloric acid (**corrosive**)

Ethanol (**highly flammable**)

Dilute nitric acid (**corrosive**)

Dilute sodium hydroxide (**corrosive**)

Silver nitrate solution, approximately 0.1 mol dm⁻³ (4 g in 250 cm³)

Sodium bromide solution, approximately 0.1 mol dm⁻³ (2.5 g in 250 cm³)

Time required 4 hours

Introduction

In this practical you will prepare 1-bromobutane in as high a yield and as pure a state as possible. You will meet several of the experimental techniques commonly used in the preparation of an organic liquid. Having prepared a sample of 1-bromobutane, you will investigate some of its chemical reactions.

Principle

Halogenoalkanes are normally prepared from their corresponding alcohol by a nucleophilic substitution reaction. The usual reagents are hydrogen halides or phosphorus halides (e.g. PCl_5, PCl_3).

> **1** Draw the structure of the alcohol from which you would make 1-bromobutane, and indicate which bond must be broken.

Hydrogen halides and phosphorus halides show acidic properties. Alcohols are weakly basic, because the lone pair on the −OH group can bond to H^+:

$$R-\overset{..}{O}H + H^+ \longrightarrow R-\overset{+}{\underset{\overset{|}{H}}{O}}-H$$

> **2** Acidic conditions make the R−O bond break more readily. Explain why.

In this preparation you will use a mixture of concentrated sulphuric acid and bromide ions instead of hydrogen bromide. The mechanism is the same as if you used hydrogen bromide, except that the initial protonation of the −OH group is by H_2SO_4 rather than HBr.

You will be preparing 1-bromobutane by the reaction of butan-1-ol with a mixture of sodium bromide and concentrated sulphuric acid. The 1-bromo-butane prepared in this way will be impure, even after distilling it off from the reaction mixture, and a lot of your time will be spent in purifying the crude product. Impurities will include:

- unreacted butan-1-ol
- oxides and oxyacids of sulphur
- bromine
- hydrogen bromide
- water

- butoxybutane
- but-1-ene.

Butan-1-ol is soluble in concentrated hydrochloric acid, so the first stage of purification is to shake with this reagent. Excess hydrochloric acid and other acidic impurities are then removed by shaking with a base, sodium hydrogencarbonate. The 1-bromobutane is then dried using anhydrous sodium sulphate, and finally distilled to remove remaining impurities.

Procedure

HIGHLY FLAMMABLE
Butan-1-ol
Bromobutane

EYE PROTECTION MUST BE WORN

HARMFUL
Butan-1-ol

VERY CORROSIVE
Concentrated sulphuric acid

IRRITANT
Bromobutane

Preparation of 1-bromobutane

CARE!
Eye protection must be worn throughout this practical.

Put 10 g of sodium bromide, 7.5 cm^3 (6 g) of butan-1-ol and 10 cm^3 of water in a 50 cm^3 pear-shaped flask. The mass of butan-1-ol used should be known so that you can calculate your final percentage yield. Fit the flask with a reflux condenser, and place a funnel in the top as shown in figure 1.

Surround the flask with a beaker of cold water to cool it during the addition of concentrated sulphuric acid. Put 10 cm^3 of this acid in the tap funnel (**CARE**). Gradually add it to the reaction mixture, carefully swirling the apparatus from time to time to mix well.

Remove the funnel from the reflux condenser and the flask from the water bath. Set the apparatus over a tripod and gauze and heat gently over a low bunsen flame so that the mixture refluxes gently for 30–45 minutes. The flask now contains crude 1-bromobutane, which must be distilled from the reaction mixture.

Allow the flask to cool and rearrange the apparatus for distillation as shown in figure 2. (The thermometer is not essential at this stage.) Boil the mixture in the flask and collect the distillate in a measuring cylinder. A form of 'steam distillation' takes place – bromobutane and water distil simultaneously and form separate layers in the measuring cylinder. Continue the distillation until the upper organic layer in the flask has disappeared. Dismantle, then clean and dry your apparatus.

The distillate in the measuring cylinder has an organic and an aqueous layer. Before the bromobutane in the organic layer can be purified, the aqueous layer must be removed and discarded. In order to avoid discarding the wrong layer, you must think carefully which layer is

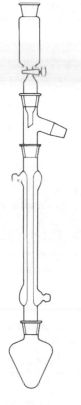

Figure 1
Apparatus for refluxing with addition.

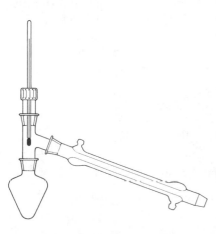

Figure 2
Apparatus for distillation.

which. One way to decide is by using the densities given in table 1. If you are still not sure which is the aqueous layer, run in a few drops of water and note which layer they enter.

Liquid	Density/g cm^{-3}
Water	1.0
Butan-1-ol	0.8
1-Bromobutane	1.3
Concentrated hydrochloric acid	1.2

Table 1

Use a teat pipette to remove the water layer. You now need to shake the crude product with concentrated hydrochloric acid to remove unreacted butanol.

CORROSIVE
Concentrated
hydrochloric acid

**EYE PROTECTION
MUST BE WORN**

CARE!
Eye protection must be worn.

Put the organic layer in a small tap funnel then pour 10 cm^3 of concentrated hydrochloric acid into the measuring cylinder you used to receive the distillate – this will wash out any traces of the crude product. Pour the acid into the tap funnel. Stopper the funnel and shake well, releasing the pressure occasionally (**CARE**). Allow the two layers to separate, decide which is the acid layer and discard it. Run the organic layer into a clean measuring cylinder.

You must now remove excess hydrogen chloride and other acid impurities by shaking with a base. Put the 1-bromobutane in a clean tap funnel. Rinse out the measuring cylinder with 10 cm^3 of sodium hydrogencarbonate solution, and pour this into the tap funnel. Stopper and shake the funnel cautiously, **regularly releasing pressure caused by the formation of carbon dioxide**. Allow the layers to separate, decide which is the 1-bromobutane layer and run it into a 50 cm^3 round flask.

The 1-bromobutane is cloudy because of the presence of water. You need to dry it. Add anhydrous sodium sulphate in small quantities, swirling after each addition, until the liquid is perfectly clear.

Finally the 1-bromobutane must be distilled to remove any remaining organic impurities. Set up the apparatus for distillation and transfer the bromobutane to the distillation flask, making sure that the sodium sulphate remains behind. Distil the 1-bromobutane, collecting the fraction with boiling range 100–104 °C (the boiling point of 1-bromobutane is 102 °C). Find the mass of 1-bromobutane collected.

3 Write a balanced equation for the overall reaction.

4 Calculate the maximum mass of 1-bromobutane that could be formed from the 6 g of butan-1-ol you used.

5 Calculate your percentage yield of 1-bromobutane.

6 In the first stage of the preparation, why are the reagents added in the particular order suggested?

7 Why is butan-1-ol much more soluble in concentrated hydrochloric acid than in water?

8 Why is sodium hydrogencarbonate used to remove acid impurities, rather than a stronger base like sodium hydroxide?

9 Outline the mechanism of the reaction between hydrogen bromide and an alcohol to produce a bromoalkane. *Chemistry in Context*, Fifth Edition, Section 29.4 will help you.

10 The preparation of 2-bromo-2-methylpropane (an isomer of 1-bromobutane) by a similar method requires much less severe conditions than the preparation here. Standing at room temperature for 20 minutes gives a good yield. Suggest a reason for this difference in the light of your proposed mechanism.

11 Give one example of an alternative preparation of monohalogenoalkanes that does not involve a substitution reaction. Could this method be readily applied to the preparation of 1-bromobutane? Explain.

Reactions of 1-bromobutane

Experiment 1:

Action of aqueous silver ions

EYE PROTECTION MUST BE WORN

1-Bromobutane is insoluble in water. In order to investigate its effect on aqueous silver ions, ethanol is used as a mutual solvent, since it dissolves both silver ions and 1-bromobutane.

Add a few drops of 1-bromobutane to 2 cm^3 of ethanol, then add 2 cm^3 of aqueous silver nitrate. Observe the reaction mixture for a few minutes. Repeat the experiment using sodium bromide solution instead of the solution of 1-bromobutane in ethanol.

12 What does this experiment suggest about the way bromine is bonded in:

  a 1-bromobutane,
  b sodium bromide?

13 What happens when the 1-bromobutane is left to stand for a few minutes in the presence of aqueous silver ions? Why does this happen?

Experiment 2:

Reaction with hydroxide ions

CORROSIVE
Dilute sodium hydroxide
Dilute nitric acid

Put 2 cm^3 of dilute sodium hydroxide solution in a test tube. Add a few drops of 1-bromobutane and warm very gently. Acidify with dilute nitric acid to neutralise the sodium hydroxide and then add 2 cm^3 of silver nitrate solution.

14 What happens? How do hydroxide ions react with 1-bromobutane?

15 Why must the sodium hydroxide be neutralised before adding silver nitrate solution?

16 Predict the products of reactions between 1-bromobutane and

a ammonia,
b ethoxide ions, $CH_3CH_2O^-$,
c cyanide ions, CN^-.

17 What type of reactions are occurring in questions **14** and **16**?

See
Investigation L10

Practical 29

Nucleophilic substitution reactions of halogenoalkanes

REQUIREMENTS

Each student, or pair of students, will need:

Eye protection

Rack and 9 test tubes

Labels

Beaker (250 cm³)

Thermometer (0 °C–100 °C)

Measuring cylinder (10 cm³)

Stop clock

1-Chlorobutane* (**highly flammable**)

1-Bromobutane* (**flammable** and **irritant**)

1-Iodobutane* (**flammable**)

2-Bromobutane* (**highly flammable**)

2-Bromo-2-methylpropane* (**highly flammable** and **harmful**)

Ethanol (**highly flammable**)

Silver nitrate solution, approximately 0.1 mol dm⁻³ (dissolve 4.25 g in distilled water and make up to 250 cm³)

Sodium iodide

Propanone (acetone) (**highly flammable** and **irritant**)

* With a separate dropping pipette for each bottle

Time required   1 hour

HIGHLY FLAMMABLE
Ethanol
1-Chlorobutane
1-Bromobutane
1-Iodobutane

IRRITANT
1-Bromobutane

EYE PROTECTION MUST BE WORN

Introduction

In this practical you will investigate the factors affecting the rate of nucleophilic substitution reactions. You will need to be familiar with the mechanism of nucleophilic substitution reactions. This is covered in *Chemistry in Context*, Fifth Edition, Section 29.4.

Procedure

Experiment 1:
Effect of the halogen atom on the rate of hydrolysis

In this experiment you will compare the rates of hydrolysis of 1-chlorobutane, 1-bromobutane and 1-iodobutane.

$$CH_3CH_2CH_2CH_2Hal + H_2O \rightarrow CH_3CH_2CH_2CH_2OH + H^+ + Hal^-$$

The rate of the reaction can be followed by carrying it out in the presence of silver ions. The halogenoalkanes, being covalently bonded, give no precipitate of silver halide. However, as the reaction proceeds and halide ions are produced, a precipitate of silver halide gradually appears:

$$Ag^+(aq) + Hal^-(aq) \rightarrow AgHal(s)$$

Halogenoalkanes are insoluble in water, so the reaction is carried out in the presence of ethanol, which acts as a mutual solvent for both the halogenoalkane and the silver ions.

> **CARE!**
> *Eye protection must be worn. Ethanol is highly flammable. Do not have any naked flames near the tubes or the ethanol bottle.*

Set up three labelled test tubes as described in table 1.

Tube 1	Tube 2	Tube 3
1 cm³ ethanol 2 drops 1-chlorobutane	1 cm³ ethanol 2 drops 1-bromobutane	1 cm³ ethanol 2 drops 1-iodobutane

Table 1
Tubes for experiment 1

Stand the tubes in a beaker of water at about 50 °C. Put a tube containing 5 cm³ of 0.1 mol dm⁻³ silver nitrate solution in the same beaker. Leave the tubes for about 10 minutes so that they reach the temperature of the bath. Add 1 cm³ of the silver nitrate solution to each of tubes 1, 2 and 3, working quickly and noting the time. Shake each tube to mix the contents and observe the tubes over the course of the next five minutes or so.

1 Which halogenoalkane undergoes hydrolysis fastest? Which is slowest?

2 Which halogenoalkane has the most polar carbon–halogen bond?

3 Is differing polarity the reason for the different rates of hydrolysis?

4 Use the bond energies shown in table 2 to suggest a possible explanation for the different rates of hydrolysis.

Bond	Average bond energy/kJ mol^{-1}
C—Cl	339
C—Br	284
C—I	218

Table 2
Average bond energies for the carbon–halogen bonds in halogenoalkanes

Experiment 2:
Effect of the structure of the carbon skeleton on the reaction mechanism and reaction rate

The experimental method is similar to that in experiment 1. In this case, instead of varying the halogen atom for a given carbon skeleton, we will vary the structure of the alkane skeleton keeping the same halogen, bromine. The bromoalkanes used are:

$$
\begin{array}{ccc}
& \text{H} & \\
CH_3CH_2CH_2\!-\!\overset{|}{\underset{|}{C}}\!-\!Br & & \\
& \text{H} &
\end{array}
\qquad
\begin{array}{c}
CH_3 \\
CH_3CH_2\!-\!\overset{|}{\underset{|}{C}}\!-\!Br \\
H
\end{array}
\qquad
\begin{array}{c}
CH_3 \\
CH_3\!-\!\overset{|}{\underset{|}{C}}\!-\!Br \\
CH_3
\end{array}
$$

       1-bromobutane   2-bromobutane   2-bromo-2-methylpropane

The general reaction is the same as in experiment 1:

$$RBr + H_2O \rightarrow ROH + H^+ + Br^-$$

(using RBr to represent the bromoalkane involved).

Tube 1	Tube 2	Tube 3
1 cm³ ethanol 2 drops 1-bromobutane	1 cm³ ethanol 2 drops 2-bromobutane	1 cm³ ethanol 2 drops 2-bromo-2-methylpropane

Table 3
Tubes for experiment 2

HIGHLY FLAMMABLE
Ethanol
1-Bromobutane
2-Bromobutane
2-Bromo-2-methylpropane

HARMFUL
2-Bromo-2-methylpropane

**EYE PROTECTION
MUST BE WORN**

Set up three labelled test tubes as described in table 3. In this experiment you will work at room temperature.

Add 1 cm³ of 0.1 mol dm⁻³ silver nitrate solution to each tube, working quickly and noting the time. Shake each tube to mix the contents. Observe the tubes over the course of the next five minutes or so.

5 Which bromoalkane is hydrolysed fastest? Which is slowest?

   Hydrolysis of halogenoalkanes proceeds by one of two mechanisms: S_N1 or S_N2 (see *Chemistry in Context*, Fifth Edition, Section 29.4).

6 Bearing in mind that the solvent in this experiment is a 1 : 1 mixture of ethanol and water (the water coming from the silver nitrate solution), which mechanism is likely to be favoured? Explain your answer.

7 Which bromoalkane would be most favoured by the mechanism you have proposed in your answer to question 6? Which would be least favoured? Explain your answer.

8 Explain the observed relative rates of hydrolysis of the three bromoalkanes.

Experiment 3:
Effect of the solvent on the reaction mechanism and the reaction rate: the Finkelstein reaction.

Experiments 1 and 2 have involved hydrolysis reactions in aqueous solution. It is, of course, impossible to carry out hydrolysis in a non-aqueous solvent! However, by using a substitution reaction known as the Finkelstein reaction you can investigate the rate of a simple nucleophilic substitution reaction in a non-aqueous solvent: propanone. The reaction is the substitution of a bromide ion by an iodide ion:

$$RBr + I^- \rightarrow RI + Br^-$$

The source of I^- is sodium iodide. Sodium iodide is soluble in propanone, but sodium bromide is not. As bromide ions are produced in the reaction, they combine with sodium ions to form a precipitate of sodium bromide.

$$RBr(pr) + Na^+(pr) + I^-(pr) \rightarrow RI(pr) + NaBr(s)$$

[(pr) indicates that the substance is in solution in propanone.]

This reaction can therefore be followed by timing the rate of appearance of the sodium bromide precipitate.

HIGHLY FLAMMABLE
Propanone

**EYE PROTECTION
MUST BE WORN**

> **CARE!**
> *Propanone is highly flammable. Do not have any naked flames near the tubes or the propanone bottle.*

Dissolve 1 g of sodium iodide in 15 cm³ of propanone. This solution is called Finkelstein's reagent.

Put 5 cm^3 of the reagent into each of three labelled test tubes and stand the tubes in a beaker of water at 35 °C. Leave the tubes for 10 minutes to reach the temperature of the water bath.

Working quickly and noting the time, add 8 drops of 1-bromobutane to the first tube, 8 drops of 2-bromobutane to the second and 8 drops of 2-bromo-2-methylpropane to the third. Observe the three tubes over the course of the next five minutes or so.

9 Which bromoalkane undergoes nucleophilic substitution by iodide ions fastest? Which is slowest?

10 Bearing in mind that the solvent in this experiment is propanone, which reaction mechanism, S_N1 or S_N2, is likely to be favoured? Explain your answer.

11 Which bromoalkane would be most favoured by the mechanism you have proposed in your answer to question 10? Which would be least favoured? Explain your answer.

12 Explain the observed order of reaction rate of the three bromoalkanes.

See
Investigation L10

Practical 30

Alcohols

REQUIREMENTS

Each student, or pair of students, will need:

Eye protection

Rack with 4 test tubes

Teat pipette

Ethanol (**highly flammable**)

Methanol (**highly flammable** and **toxic**)

Propan-2-ol (**highly flammable**)

Full range indicator paper

Sodium, cut into small rice grain-sized pieces (**highly flammable** and **corrosive**)

Small beaker (100 cm³)

Bunsen burner

Splint

Concentrated sulphuric acid (**very corrosive**)

Concentrated ('glacial') ethanoic (acetic) acid (**corrosive**)

2-Hydroxybenzoic (salicylic) acid (**harmful**)

Phosphorus pentachloride (**corrosive**)

Silver nitrate solution (about 0.1 mol dm⁻³)

Dilute sulphuric acid (**irritant**)

Potassium dichromate(VI) solution (about 1 mol dm⁻³) (**very toxic**)

About 20 cm of medium gauge copper wire wound into a spiral at one end

Access to a fume cupboard

Time required 2½ hours

Introduction

Alcohols are organic compounds with the general formula:

$$R_2 - \overset{\displaystyle R_1}{\underset{\displaystyle R_3}{C}} - OH$$

R_1, R_2 and R_3 may be hydrogen or any alkyl or aryl group. Most alcohols can be regarded as alkanes in which a hydrogen atom has been replaced by an –OH group. Examples are ethanol (CH_3CH_2OH), propan-2-ol ($CH_3CHOHCH_3$) and cyclohexanol ($C_6H_{11}OH$).

In this practical you will compare the physical properties of alcohols with those of other organic compounds of similar relative molecular mass, then look at some of their typical chemical properties.

Comparing the physical properties of alcohols, alkanes and ethers

1 Copy and complete table 1 below using a data book.

2 Explain the relative volatilities of ethanol, methoxymethane and propane.

3 Explain the relative solubilites in water of ethanol, methoxymethane and propane.

4 Why has ethanol been compared with methoxymethane and propane rather than ethoxyethane and ethane?

Compound	Relative molecular mass	Structural formula	Melting point/°C	Boiling point/°C	Relative solubility in water
Ethanol Methoxymethane Propane					

Table 1
Comparing the physical properties of ethanol, methoxymethane and propane

Investigating the chemical properties of alcohols

CARE!
Eye protection must be worn throughout this practical.

(1) Reactions in which the O–H bond breaks

Reactions of alcohols involving cleavage of the O–H bond can be compared with similar reactions for water.

Reaction with sodium

CORROSIVE
Sodium

HIGHLY FLAMMABLE
Ethanol
Sodium

Put 1 cm^3 of ethanol in a test tube and add one small, **rice grain-sized** piece of sodium. Try to identify the gas produced. **Dispose of the remaining solution carefully because it is very corrosive.**

5 Describe what happens. Is the reaction of sodium with ethanol more or less vigorous than the reaction of sodium with water?

6 Put a piece of damp indicator paper into the liquid remaining after sodium has reacted with ethanol. Describe and explain what happens.

7 Write balanced equations for the reactions of sodium with: **a** water, **b** ethanol.

8 Explain the relative reactivities of ethanol and water with sodium.

Reaction with organic acids – esterification

CORROSIVE
Glacial ethanoic acid

VERY CORROSIVE
Concentrated
sulphuric acid

**EYE PROTECTION
MUST BE WORN**

Put 10 drops of ethanol in a test tube and add 10 drops of concentrated ethanoic (acetic) acid. Carefully, add 6 drops of concentrated sulphuric acid, and then warm the mixture, without boiling for 5 minutes. Now, pour the contents of the test tube into about 50 cm^3 of water in a beaker, and smell cautiously.

9 Why must the mixture not be boiled?

10 The product, ethyl ethanoate (acetate), is an ester. Describe its smell.

11 Why does the smell of the ester become more prominent after the mixture is poured into water?

12 Write an equation for the reaction between ethanol and ethanoic acid, clearly showing the structure of the ester.

13 Why is concentrated sulphuric acid added to the reaction mixture?

14 What uses has ethyl ethanoate?

HARMFUL
2-Hydroxybenzoic
acid

Repeat the experiment using 2-hydroxybenzoic acid (salicylic acid) in place of ethanoic acid. (Use approximately equal volumes of solid 2-hydroxybenzoic acid and ethanol.)

15 What is the name of the ester produced? What does it smell like?

16 This ester is a constituent of 'oil of wintergreen'. What is this oil used for?

17 How and why has isotopic labelling been used in the study of esterification reactions? (See *Chemistry in Context*, Fifth Edition, Section 32.5).

(2) Reactions in which the C–OH bond breaks

Reaction with phosphorus halides

Phosphorus pentachloride reacts with alcohols to form alkyl chlorides.

> **CARE!**
> *The reaction produces corrosive fumes. Work in a fume cupboard.*

EYE PROTECTION MUST BE WORN

USE A FUME CUPBOARD

CORROSIVE
Phosphorus pentachloride

Add a *little* phosphorus pentachloride to 10 drops of ethanol. Collect some of the fumes evolved in a teat pipette and identify them by bubbling into silver nitrate solution.

When the fumes have subsided and the reaction is complete, pour the contents of the tube into 50 cm^3 of water in a beaker and cautiously smell the product.

18 What gas is evolved when phosphorus pentachloride reacts with ethanol?

19 Write equations for the reactions of ethanol with:

   a phosphorus pentachloride,
   b phosphorus trichloride.

Reactions with concentrated hydrohalic acids

The reactions between alcohols and concentrated hydrohalic acids (or halide ions in concentrated sulphuric acid) are important in the preparation of alkyl halides. The preparation of 1-bromobutane in practical 28 uses this procedure.

20 Write an equation or equations for the preparation of 2-bromopropane using potassium bromide, concentrated sulphuric acid and an appropriate alcohol.

(3) Reactions of the —CH$_2$OH and $>$CHOH groups

Alcohols with a —CH$_2$OH group can be oxidised first to an aldehyde containing the 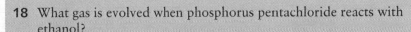 group, and then to a carboxylic acid with the 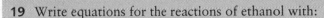 group.

alcohol   aldehyde

carboxylic
acid

Alcohols with a $\diagdown$CHOH group can be oxidised to ketones containing the $\diagdown$C = O group. Further oxidation is difficult.

alcohol   ketone

Oxidation with acidified potassium dichromate(VI)

Add 10 drops of dilute sulphuric acid and 5 drops of potassium dichromate(VI) solution to 5 drops of ethanol. Mix thoroughly and then warm the mixture. Smell cautiously.

VERY TOXIC
Potassium
dichromate(VI)
solution

IRRITANT
Dilute sulphuric acid

**EYE PROTECTION
MUST BE WORN**

> 21 Describe what happens and explain the colour changes.
>
> 22 Write equations (or half-equations) for the oxidation of ethanol.
>
> 23 What conditions and techniques would favour the oxidation of ethanol to:
>
>   **a** ethanal rather than ethanoic acid,
>   **b** ethanoic acid rather than ethanal?

Repeat the experiment using first methanol and then propan-2-ol in place of ethanol.

TOXIC
Methanol

HIGHLY FLAMMABLE
Methanol
Propan-2-ol
Ethanol

> 24 Write equations (or half-equations) for the oxidation of methanol and propan-2-ol. Name the oxidation products. (**Note:** the final oxidation products from methanol are carbon dioxide and water.)

Catalytic oxidation of alcohols

Put **10 drops only** of methanol in a test tube. (**CARE highly flammable.** There should be no naked flames nearby.) Light a bunsen well away from the methanol and heat a clean copper spiral to red heat in the roaring bunsen flame.

> 25 What do you notice as the red-hot spiral is moved out of the hot bunsen flame? Write an equation for the reaction which occurs.

Now introduce the red-hot spiral into the methanol vapour in the test tube.

26 Observe the copper spiral carefully and explain the changes in colour which take place on its surface. (**Hint**: methanol is oxidised to methanal (formaldehyde).)

27 Explain how the copper acts as a catalyst in the oxidation of methanol by air.

Industrially, methanal is manufactured by passing a mixture of methanol vapour and air over a catalyst of silver, rather than copper, at 450 °C–600 °C.

Practical 31

Phenol

REQUIREMENTS

Each student, or pair of students, will need;

Eye protection

Rack and 4 test tubes (one fitted with a stopper)

Boiling tube

Beaker (250 cm³)

Conical flask (250 cm³), fitted with a stopper

Broken porcelain or crucible

Tongs

Spatula

Evaporating basin

Melting point tube and access to apparatus for melting point determination

Glass rod

Buchner funnel and flask

Filter paper

Access to suction pump

Phenol (**toxic** and **corrosive**)

Universal indicator paper

Dilute sodium hydroxide solution (**corrosive**)

Concentrated hydrochloric acid (**corrosive**)

Concentrated sulphuric acid (**very corrosive**)

Ethanol (**highly flammable**)

Sodium metal, ready cut into pieces about the size of a grain of rice (**corrosive** and **highly flammable**)

Benzoyl chloride (keep in fume cupboard) (**corrosive**)

Bromine water (**toxic** and **corrosive**)

Iron(III) chloride solution (about 0.1 mol dm⁻³)

Benzene-1,2-dicarboxylic acid anhydride (phthalic anhydride) (**irritant**)

Access to a fume cupboard

Protective gloves

Time required

Experiments 1 to 6: $1\frac{1}{4}$ hours.

Experiment 7: $1\frac{1}{4}$ hours

Introduction

Phenol contains the same functional group as ethanol and other aliphatic alcohols. However, the benzene ring has a big effect on the behaviour of the hydroxyl group, OH, so many of the properties of phenol are very different from those of ethanol. In this practical you will examine some of the differences between these two hydroxy-compounds. You can also prepare phenyl benzoate and use some of the standard techniques for purifying a solid organic compound and testing its purity.

Phenol

Procedure

EYE PROTECTION MUST BE WORN	**WEAR PROTECTIVE GLOVES**	**USE A FUME CUPBOARD**	**CORROSIVE** Phenol	**TOXIC** Phenol

CARE!
Phenol is toxic and corrosive. Avoid all skin contact and wear protective gloves. Eye protection must be worn throughout this practical.

Experiment 1: Combustion

Working in a fume cupboard, set fire to a small crystal of phenol on a piece of broken porcelain held in tongs.

1 With what sort of flame does phenol burn?

2 What does ethanol look like when it burns?

3 Explain the differences in the flames you see when ethanol and phenol burn.

Experiment 2:
Acidic nature

Add a spatula-full of phenol to 5 cm³ of water in a test tube. Stopper the tube and shake. Remove the stopper and warm the tube in a beaker of hot water. Note what occurs, then cool the tube and again note what happens.

CORROSIVE
Sodium hydroxide
solution
Concentrated
hydrochloric acid

4 How does the solubility of phenol in water compare with that of ethanol in water?

To the cooled tube add a little dilute sodium hydroxide solution and mix thoroughly.

5 Is phenol more soluble in aqueous sodium hydroxide than in water? If so, why?

Now add a little concentrated hydrochloric acid (**CARE**).

6 Describe and explain what happens.

Make a stock solution of phenol by putting a spatula-full of phenol into a boiling tube and half-filling with water.

HIGHLY FLAMMABLE
Ethanol

Test a portion of the solution with universal indicator. For comparison, test a solution of ethanol in water with universal indicator.

7 Explain why ethanol and phenol differ in acidity.

Experiment 3:
Reaction with sodium

CORROSIVE
Sodium

HIGHLY FLAMMABLE
Sodium

Dissolve a few crystals of phenol in a few cubic centimetres of ethanol. **Working in a fume cupboard,** put the solution in an evaporating basin and add a piece of sodium **about the size of a grain of rice (CARE).** Observe the reaction and try to decide what is formed. Compare the reaction with that of a similar-sized piece of sodium with ethanol alone. **Destroy any sodium left over, in excess ethanol.**

8 Write an equation for the reaction of phenol with sodium.
9 Use your knowledge of the relative acid strengths of phenol and ethanol to explain the difference in the reaction of sodium with the two compounds.

Experiment 4:
Complexing reactions

Add a few drops of iron(III) chloride solution to an aqueous solution of phenol. Repeat the reaction using ethanol instead of phenol.

10 Describe the characteristic colour given by phenol and Fe^{3+}(aq).

11 What is the cause of this colour?

Experiment 5:
Substitution reactions of phenol

VERY TOXIC
Bromine water

CORROSIVE
Bromine water

**EYE PROTECTION
MUST BE WORN**

Add bromine water drop by drop to an aqueous solution of phenol, until it is present in excess.

12 What happens?

13 Use *Chemistry in Context*, Fifth edition, Section 30.8 to find the formula of the product, and write an equation for the reaction.

14 Ethanol has no reaction with bromine water. Explain the difference between the two compounds in this respect.

Experiment 6:
Preparation of phenolphthalein

The indicator phenolphthalein can be prepared by the reaction between phenol and benzene-1,2-dicarboxylic anhydride (phthalic anhydride):

**WEAR PROTECTIVE
GLOVES**

**EYE PROTECTION
MUST BE WORN**

VERY CORROSIVE
Concentrated
sulphuric acid
Sodium hydroxide
solution

IRRITANT
Benzene-1,2-
dicarboxylic anhydride

benzene-1,2-dicarboxylic
anhydride
(phthalic anhydride) + 2 phenol → phenolphthalein $+ H_2O$

Mix 0.5 g of phenol and 0.5 g of benzene-1,2-dicarboxylic anhydride in a test tube. Heat the mixture with 1 drop of concentrated sulphuric acid (**CARE**). Cool and then **carefully** add a little dilute sodium hydroxide solution. Investigate the colour change that occurs when the solution is acidified.

15 Phenolphthalein is a weak acid which dissociates in the following way:

⇌ H^+ +

Experiment 7:
Esterification: preparation of phenyl benzoate

Phenol differs from ethanol in the ease with which it forms esters. Ethanol readily forms ethyl esters by heating it with a carboxylic acid in the presence of concentrated sulphuric acid. However, phenol does not form phenyl esters so readily.

Phenyl benzoate, for example, cannot be prepared by heating phenol with benzoic acid and concentrated sulphuric acid. The benzoic acid must be activated by converting it to benzoyl chloride. This readily reacts with phenol in basic conditions to give a good yield of phenyl benzoate.

phenol   benzoyl   phenyl benzoate
      chloride

16 Why is phenol more difficult to esterify than ethanol?

17 Why is benzoyl chloride effective in esterifying phenol?

In the experiment which follows you will prepare phenyl benzoate in this way and, if you have time, purify your sample and check its purity by measuring its melting point.

CARE!
Benzoyl chloride is corrosive and its vapour irritates the eyes. Avoid spilling the liquid. Do not release its vapour outside the fume cupboard.

Fit a 250 cm^3 conical flask with a stopper, **which must fit tightly so reagents cannot leak out of the flask**. Put 5 g of phenol in the flask. Add 90 cm^3 of 2 mol dm^{-3} sodium hydroxide solution. **Working in a fume cupboard**, carefully add 9 cm^3 of benzoyl chloride.

Put the stopper in the flask and shake vigorously. Leave for 10 minutes, shaking from time to time. Phenyl benzoate separates out as white crystals.

Purifying phenyl benzoate

Filter off the crystals using a Buchner funnel. Work in a fume cupboard because some unreacted benzoyl chloride may still be present. Wash the crystals several times with water, breaking up any lumps using a glass rod.

The crystals can now be purified by recrystallisation. Dissolve them in the minimum possible quantity of ethanol in a boiling tube, heating the

CORROSIVE
Sodium hydroxide solution

EYE PROTECTION MUST BE WORN

USE A FUME CUPBOARD

IRRITANT
Benzoyl chloride vapour

CORROSIVE
Benzoyl chloride

HIGHLY FLAMMABLE
Ethanol

ethanol in a water-bath at about 60 °C. **There must be no flames nearby. Get the hot water from a tap or kettle**. Now allow the solution to cool so that the crystals separate out and can be filtered off, leaving impurities behind in the solution.

Filter off the crystals using a Buchner funnel. Dry the crystals between filter papers.

The purity of your sample can be assessed by measuring its melting point. Seal a melting point tube at one end, then put into it a few crystals of your sample. The tube must now be heated slowly until the sample melts, at which point the temperature is noted. To do this you may use an electrical melting point apparatus or hot oil – your teacher will show you the details of whichever method you are to use. Remember to heat the tube very slowly, otherwise you may 'overshoot' and get an inaccurate value for the melting point.

18 Record the melting point of your crystals. The melting point of pure phenyl benzoate is 71 °C.

19 What can you say about the purity of your own sample?

20 Summarise the main differences between phenol and ethanol.

Practical 32

Carbonyl compounds

REQUIREMENTS

Each student, or pair of students, will require:

Eye protection

Rack with 4 test tubes

Propanal (propionaldehyde) (**highly flammable** and **irritant**)

Aqueous methanal (40% solution–formalin) (**toxic** and **corrosive**)

Propanone (acetone) (**irritant** and **highly flammable**)

Glucose

Saturated sodium hydrogensulphite solution (**harmful**)

Concentrated sodium hydroxide solution (**corrosive**) (Dissolve 30 g of NaOH (**corrosive**) in 100 cm^3 of water.)

Ice

Salt

Hydrogen chloride generator (**toxic** and **corrosive**) (Add concentrated sulphuric acid (**very corrosive**) to sodium chloride (rock salt).)

2,4-Dinitrophenylhydrazine solution–Brady's reagent (Dissolve 2 g of 2,4-dinitrophenylhydrazine (**toxic, and explosive when dry**) in 4 cm^3 of concentrated sulphuric acid (**very corrosive**) and add carefully, with cooling, 30 cm^3 of methanol (**highly flammable, toxic**). Warm gently to dissolve any undissolved solid and then add 10 cm^3 of water.

2 mol dm^{-3} sulphuric acid (**corrosive**)

Ethanol (**highly flammable**)

The following solutions:

- potassium dichromate(VI) (about 0.1 mol dm^{-3}) (**toxic**)

- silver nitrate (about 0.1 mol dm^{-3})

- dilute ammonia

- Fehling's solution (Mix equal volumes of solutions A and B. Store solutions A and B separately because the mixture will deteriorate.)

- solution A Dissolve 17 g of CuSO$_4$.5H$_2$O in 250 cm^3 of water.

- solution B (**corrosive**) Dissolve 86 g of potassium sodium tartrate (Rochelle salt) and 30g of NaOH (**corrosive**) in 250 cm^3 of water. Warming may be necessary.

(Contd.)

Introduction

Carbonyl compounds contain the carbonyl group, $\diagup\text{C}=\text{O}$, which is the functional group in both aldehydes such as propanal (propionaldehyde) and ketones such as propanone (acetone). The reactions of the carbonyl group are important to organic chemists, as the group is common in biological molecules, particularly carbohydrates such as glucose and ribose. Carbonyl compounds are also used in the manufacture of plastics and as organic solvents.

The double bond between C and O in the carbonyl group, like the double bond in alkenes, consists of a σ-bond and a π-bond. Unlike the C=C group, however, the carbonyl group does not have an even electron distribution between the two atoms and there is a greater electron density near the more electronegative oxygen atom (figure 1).

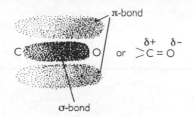

Figure 1
Electron density in the carbonyl bond.

In this practical, you will compare the properties of two aldehydes, methanal and propanal, and a ketone, propanone.

$$\underset{\text{methanal}}{\overset{\text{H}}{\underset{\text{O}}{\diagup\text{C}\diagdown}}\text{H}} \qquad \underset{\text{propanal}}{\overset{\text{CH}_3\text{CH}_2}{\underset{\text{O}}{\diagup\text{C}\diagdown}}\text{H}} \qquad \underset{\text{propanone}}{\overset{\text{CH}_3}{\underset{\text{O}}{\diagup\text{C}\diagdown}}\text{CH}_3}$$

A   Addition reactions of carbonyl compounds

The electron distribution in the carbonyl bond makes the carbon atom attractive towards nucleophiles which attack and bond to it, breaking the π-bond and resulting in addition. With a general nucleophile, $\ddot{\text{X}}$–Y:

$$\underset{\ddot{\text{X}}-\text{Y}}{\overset{\delta+}{\diagup\text{C}}}\overset{\delta-}{=\text{O}} \longrightarrow \underset{\text{X}}{\diagup}\text{C}\overset{\text{O}^-}{\diagdown} + \text{Y}^+ \longrightarrow \underset{\text{X}}{\diagup}\text{C}\overset{\text{OY}}{\diagdown}$$

This is **nucleophilic addition**. The mechanism is covered in detail in *Chemistry in Context*, Fifth Edition, Section 31.3.

Teat pipette

Watch glass

Small beaker (150 cm³ or 250 cm³)

Bunsen burner

Tripod

Gauze

Filter paper

Melting point tubes

Access to melting point apparatus

Access to fume cupboard

Time required   2–3 hours

HARMFUL
Sodium
hydrogensulphite
solution

IRRITANT
Propanone
Propanal

**HIGHLY
FLAMMABLE**
Propanone
Propanal

**EYE PROTECTION
MUST BE WORN**

1 Bearing in mind that the first stage of addition involves attack on the $C^{\delta+}$, predict the relative reactivity of methanal, propanal and propanone. (**Hint:** The methyl group is electron-donating in these compounds.)

CARE!
Eye protection must be worn throughout this practical.

Reactions with sodium hydrogensulphite

To 2 cm³ of propanone, add 1 cm³ of saturated sodium hydrogensulphite solution, $NaHSO_3(aq)$, a little at a time. Shake thoroughly to ensure mixing after each addition. Judge whether a reaction has taken place by seeing if it gets hot. Cool the mixture in a stream of cold water to encourage crystallisation of any solid product.

2 Describe what happens during this reaction.

3 Draw a full structural formula for the hydrogensulphite ion.

4 Write an equation for the reaction of propanone with sodium hydrogensulphite.

Repeat the experiment using propanal in place of propanone. Describe what happens.

5 Why are these carbonyl hydrogensulphite addition compounds fairly soluble in water?

6 Carbonyl hydrogensulph*ate* compounds (hydrogensulphate ion is HSO_4^-) are more difficult to prepare than carbonyl hydrogensulph*ite* compounds. Suggest why.

B   Condensation reactions of carbonyl compounds

In some cases, the addition reactions of carbonyl compounds are followed by the elimination of a molecule of water. Many of these elimination reactions involve derivatives of ammonia with the general formula $X-NH_2$.

$$\diagup_{\diagdown}C=O + H_2N-X \longrightarrow \begin{array}{c} OH \\ | \\ -C-N \\ | \end{array}\begin{array}{c} H \\ \diagup \\ \diagdown \\ X \end{array} \longrightarrow \diagup_{\diagdown}C=N_{\diagdown X} + H_2O$$

This sort of reaction, in which two molecules combine with the elimination of water, is an example of a **condensation** or **addition–elimination** reaction.

The most useful reagent for low molecular mass carbonyl compounds is 2,4-dinitrophenylhydrazine (2,4-DNP):

The products of condensation reactions between 2,4-dinitrophenylhydrazine and carbonyl compounds are crystalline solids with well-defined melting points. Because of this, they are useful in identifying individual carbonyl compounds. You prepare the condensation compound with 2,4-dinitrophenylhydrazine then compare its melting point with data book values.

Preparation of propanone 2,4-dinitrophenylhydrazone

Add 5 cm^3 of 2,4-dinitrophenylhydrazine solution (sometimes called Brady's reagent) to 3 drops of propanone. If crystals do not form, add a little 2 mol dm^{-3} sulphuric acid, warm the mixture and then cool in iced water.

If you have time, you can purify the crystals and measure their melting point. Filter off the crystals, wash them with a little water, dry them between filter papers and then recrystallise them from ethanol. Determine their melting point and compare your value with the accepted value of 128 °C for the melting point of propanone 2,4-dinitrophenylhydrazone.

EYE PROTECTION MUST BE WORN

TOXIC
2,4-Dinitrophenylhydrazine

HIGHLY FLAMMABLE
Ethanol
2,4-Dinitrophenylhydrazine solution

CORROSIVE
Sulphuric acid

7 Describe the appearance of propanone 2,4-dinitrophenylhydrazone crystals.

8 Write an equation for the reaction between propanone and 2,4-dinitrophenylhydrazine.

Other carbonyl compounds react in a similar manner to propanone.

C Oxidation of carbonyl compounds

Aldehydes have a hydrogen atom attached to their carbonyl group. This hydrogen is activated by the carbonyl group and is readily oxidised to –OH. Aldehydes are therefore readily oxidised to carboxylic acids.

Ketones, however, have no hydrogen atom joined directly to the carbonyl group, so they are not readily oxidised.

9 What would you expect to be the relative ease of oxidation of methanal, propanal and propanone?

IRRITANT
Sulphuric acid

CORROSIVE
Methanal

TOXIC
Methanal
Potassium
dichromate(VI)
solution

**EYE PROTECTION
MUST BE WORN**

HIGHLY FLAMMABLE
Propanal
Propanone

(1) Oxidation by acidified dichromate(VI)

Compare the ease of oxidation and hence the reducing power of methanal, propanal and propanone. Add 5 drops of a solution of methanal in water to a mixture of 2 drops of potassium dichromate(VI) solution and 10 drops of dilute sulphuric acid. If nothing happens in the cold, warm gently.

Repeat the test, using 5 drops of propanal in place of the methanal solution. Finally, repeat using 5 drops of propanone.

10 Write the carbonyl compounds (methanal, propanal and propanone) in order of increasing reducing power. Do your results agree with your answer to question 9?

11 Write equations (or half-equations) for the reactions which have occurred.

(2) Oxidation by diamminosilver(I) ions (Tollen's reagent)

Put 3 cm^3 of silver nitrate solution into a *clean* test tube and add dilute ammonia solution drop by drop until the precipitate of silver oxide just dissolves. The clear solution contains $[Ag(NH_3)_2]^+$ ions. Add 10 drops of propanal and warm the resulting mixture in a beaker of hot water. **Rinse out the test tube immediately afterwards, because the mixture is explosive when dry.**

12 Describe and explain what happens. Write an equation (or half-equations) for the reaction which occurs.

Repeat the experiment using first methanal and then propanone in place of propanal.

13 How do the reactions of methanal and propanone compare with that of propanal?

(3) Oxidation by Fehling's solution (copper(II) ions complexed with tartrate ions)

CORROSIVE
Fehling's solution

Put 3 cm^3 of Fehling's solution in a boiling tube and add 10 drops of propanal. Boil the mixture gently and note the formation of orange-red copper(I) oxide.

14 Fehling's solution contains Cu^{2+} ions in an alkaline solution of tartrate ions. The tartrate ions complex with Cu^{2+} ions and prevent the precipitation of copper(II) hydroxide. Describe and explain what happens when propanal reacts with Fehling's solution. Write an equation (or half-equations) for the reaction which occurs. (In your equation represent the complexed copper(II) ion as Cu^{2+} for simplicity.)

15 How would you expect:

   a methanal
   b propanone

to react with Fehling's solution?

D   Sugars–naturally occurring carbonyl compounds

Sugars are sweet-tasting soluble carbohydrates.

The most obvious feature of their structures is the presence of large numbers of –OH groups.

16 What do you understand by the term 'carbohydrate'?

17 Why are sugars very soluble in water?

As well as showing the properties of hydroxy compounds, sugars such as glucose show many properties that are typical of carbonyl compounds. The carbonyl properties of glucose arise from the fact that it can exist in an 'open-chain' form as well as its normal 'ring' form, as shown below. In aqueous solution about 1% of glucose molecules exist in the open-chain form which carries the aldehyde group.

ring form   open-chain form

(1) Condensation with 2,4-dinitrophenylhydrazine

EYE PROTECTION MUST BE WORN

Carry out the experiment in part **B** (condensation reactions of carbonyl compounds), using half a spatula measure of glucose in 1 cm^3 of water in place of 3 drops of propanone.

18 Describe the appearance of the crystals which form, and write an equation for the reaction between glucose and 2,4-dinitrophenylhydrazine. (Use the open-chain formula for glucose in this equation.)

(2) Oxidation by diamminosilver(I) ions (Tollen's reagent)

Carry out experiment 2, in part C (oxidation of carbonyl compounds), using half a spatula measure of glucose in 1 cm^3 of water in place of 10 drops of propanal. **Rinse out the test tube immediately after the reaction.**

19 Describe and explain what happens.

(3) Oxidation by Fehling's solution

Fehling's test has been used to detect sugar in the urine of people suffering from diabetes. Sugar can accumulate in the blood of diabetics and, when it reaches a certain concentration, it is excreted by the kidneys and appears in the urine.

Carry out experiment 3, in part C, using half a spatula measure of glucose in 1 cm^3 of water in place of 10 drops of propanal.

20 Describe and explain what happens. Depending on the concentration of glucose, the solution may simply turn green, or produce a fine yellow precipitate or give a dark red precipitate.

Practical 33

Carboxylic acids

REQUIREMENTS

Each student, or pair of students, will require:

Eye protection

Rack and 6 hard-glass test tubes

2 boiling tubes

Evaporating basin

Beaker (250 cm³)

Dropping pipette

Splints

Universal indicator paper (pH 1 to 4 or full range 1 to 14) or, better, access to a pH meter

Access to a refrigerator

Access to a fume cupboard

Concentrated (glacial) ethanoic (acetic) acid (**corrosive**)

Concentrated methanoic (formic) acid (**corrosive**)

Solid ethanedioic acid (oxalic acid) (**harmful**)

2 mol dm⁻³ ethanoic acid (**irritant**) (dilute 116 cm³ of concentrated ethanoic acid (**corrosive**) to 1 dm³ with distilled water)

0.1 mol dm⁻³ ethanoic acid (dilute 5.8 cm³ of concentrated ethanoic acid to 1 dm³ with distilled water)

0.1 mol dm⁻³ ethanol in water (dilute 1.5 cm³ of ethanol (**highly flammable**) to 250 cm³ with distilled water)

0.1 mol dm⁻³ hydrochloric acid (dilute 8.6 cm³ of concentrated acid (**corrosive**) to 1 dm³ with distilled water)

Phosphorus pentachloride (**corrosive:** keep in fume cupboard)

Pentanol (amyl alcohol) (**harmful and flammable**)

Concentrated sulphuric acid (**very corrosive**)

Ethanol (**highly flammable**)

Dilute sodium hydroxide (**corrosive**)

Dilute hydrochloric acid (**irritant**)

Dilute ammonia solution (**irritant**)

Potassium manganate(VII) (potassium permanganate) solution (0.1 mol dm⁻³)

Iron(III) chloride (ferric chloride) solution (0.1 mol dm⁻³)

Sodium ethanoate solution (0.1 mol dm⁻³)

Time required $2\frac{1}{2}$ – 4 hours

Introduction

Carboxylic acids contain the functional group $-C\begin{smallmatrix}OH\\\\O\end{smallmatrix}$ They have important industrial uses, and occur widely in nature, both free and combined as esters, particularly in fats and oils.

In this practical you will begin by considering some of the properties of ethanoic acid, a typical carboxylic acid, and then look at some of the unusual properties of methanoic acid and ethanedioic acid. The structural formulae of these acids are shown in table 1.

Systematic name	Other name	Structural formula	
Methanoic acid	Formic acid	$H-C\begin{smallmatrix}O\\\\OH\end{smallmatrix}$	HCOOH
Ethanoic acid	Acetic acid	$CH_3-C\begin{smallmatrix}O\\\\OH\end{smallmatrix}$	CH₃COOH
Ethanedioic acid	Oxalic acid	$\begin{smallmatrix}O\\\\HO\end{smallmatrix}C-C\begin{smallmatrix}O\\\\OH\end{smallmatrix}$	(COOH)₂

Table 1
Structural formulae of methanoic, ethanoic and ethanedioic acids

Procedure

CARE! Eye protection must be worn throughout this practical.	**EYE PROTECTION MUST BE WORN**	**CORROSIVE** Concentrated ethanoic acid

(1) The Properties of ethanoic acid as a typical carboxylic acid

CARE!
Concentrated (glacial) ethanoic acid is corrosive. Any spill should be washed away immediately with plenty of water.

Experiment 1:
Physical properties of concentrated ('glacial') ethanoic acid

Put a stoppered test tube of concentrated ethanoic acid in a refrigerator and observe after an hour.

> 1 What happens? Why is concentrated ethanoic acid called 'glacial'?

Cautiously smell the vapour from a bottle of concentrated ethanoic acid. Hold the bottle at a distance, fill your lungs with air and waft the vapour towards your nose.

> 2 Is the smell familiar? How did the original name 'acetic acid' come to be used for what we now call ethanoic acid?

Test the solubility of concentrated ethanoic acid in water.

> 3 Is the acid soluble in water? Explain your answer in terms of the structure of the acid.
>
> 4 Would you expect octadecanoic acid, $C_{17}H_{35}COOH$ to be soluble in water? Explain your answer.

Experiment 2:
Acidic properties of ethanoic acid

EYE PROTECTION MUST BE WORN

Using universal indicator paper, or preferably a pH meter, measure the pH of 0.1 mol dm^{-3} solutions of:

a ethanol,

b ethanoic acid,

c hydrochloric acid.

> 5 Record your results and list the three compounds in order of increasing acid strength.
>
> 6 Would you classify ethanoic acid as a strong or a weak acid?
>
> 7 What explanation can you give for the difference in acid strength between ethanol and ethanoic acid?

Measure the pH of a 0.1 mol dm^{-3} solution of sodium ethanoate.

> 8 Why might sodium ethanoate be expected to be neutral?
>
> 9 Is it neutral in fact? If not, why not?

CORROSIVE
Sodium hydroxide solution

Put 10 cm^3 of 2 mol dm^{-3} sodium hydroxide solution in an evaporating basin. Add 5 cm^3 of 2 mol dm^{-3} ethanoic acid and **cautiously** smell the resulting mixture.

> 10 Can ethanoic acid still be smelled? If not, why not?

IRRITANT
Dilute ethanoic acid
Dilute hydrochloric acid

Add a further 5 cm^3 or so of 2 mol dm^{-3} ethanoic acid to the evaporating basin, until the acid is just in excess. (How can you test whether it is in excess?) Evaporate the contents of the evaporating basin over a beaker of boiling water until all the water has left the basin and white crystals remain. (This may take some time. Get on with another part of the practical while you are waiting.)

> **11** Identify the white crystals and write an equation for the reaction that has occurred.

Put a few of the crystals in a test tube and add a few cubic centimetres of dilute hydrochloric acid. Gently warm the tube and **cautiously** smell the vapour coming off.

> **12** What has been formed? Explain the reaction that has occurred in terms of your answer to question 5.

Experiment 3:
Reaction of ethanoic acid with phosphorus pentachloride

> ### CARE!
> *Phosphorus pentachloride is corrosive and reacts violently with water. Do not let it come into contact with water, and avoid spills. Stopper the reagent bottle immediately after use.*

USE A FUME CUPBOARD

CORROSIVE
Phosphorus pentachloride
Concentrated ethanoic acid

EYE PROTECTION MUST BE WORN

Working in a fume cupboard, put 2 cm^3 of **concentrated** ethanoic acid in a boiling tube. Carefully add about 0.5 g of phosphorus pentachloride.

> **13** What evidence is there that a reaction has occurred?
>
> **14** Give the formula of the organic product of this reaction and write an equation. (Consult *Chemistry in Context*, Fifth Edition, Section 32.4 if necessary.)
>
> **15** How would you expect phosphorus pentachloride to react with *ethanol*? How does this reaction resemble the reaction of phosphorus pentachloride with ethanoic acid?

Experiment 4:
Reaction of ethanoic acid and ethanoates with neutral iron(III) chloride

USE A FUME CUPBOARD

EYE PROTECTION MUST BE WORN

Aqueous Fe^{3+} ions give a characteristic colour with ethanoate ions, but only in neutral solution.

Iron(III) chloride solution is normally acidic. Prepare a neutral solution as follows. Add ammonia solution drop by drop to a few cubic centimetres of iron(III) chloride solution, until a faint precipitate just begins to form. Filter or decant the solution from the precipitate and then, **working in a fume cupboard**, gently warm the solution to drive off excess ammonia. You now have a neutral solution of iron(III) chloride.

Put 2–3 cm³ of sodium ethanoate solution in a test tube and add a few drops of neutral iron(III) chloride solution. (Sodium ethanoate is used here instead of ethanoic acid because it is nearly neutral.)

16 What colour is given by ethanoate ions with neutral iron(III) chloride?

17 What other organic compounds give a characteristic colour with iron(III) chloride? What colour do they give?

Experiment 5:
Esterification

FLAMMABLE
Pentanol

HARMFUL
Pentanol

VERY CORROSIVE
Concentrated sulphuric acid
Concentrated ethanoic acid

**EYE PROTECTION
MUST BE WORN**

Put 2 cm³ of pentanol (amyl alcohol) in a boiling tube and add 1 cm³ of concentrated sulphuric acid. Add a few drops of concentrated ethanoic acid and warm the tube gently with shaking (**CARE**). Allow the tube to cool a little, then pour the contents into a beaker containing about 50 cm³ of cold water. **Cautiously** smell the vapour.

18 Describe the smell of the vapour.

19 The pentanol you used may have been a mixture of isomers of formula $C_5H_{11}OH$. Using pentan-1-ol as a representative example, name and write the structural formula of the ester that has been formed.

20 Write an equation for the reaction.

21 What is the purpose of the sulphuric acid in this reaction?

22 Why is the reaction mixture poured into cold water before smelling?

23 Give the names and structural formulae of the esters that would have been formed if:

   a ethanol had been used instead of pentanol,
   b propanoic acid had been used instead of ethanoic acid.

TOXIC
Potassium
manganate(VII)

Experiment 6:
Oxidation

Put 2 cm³ of concentrated ethanoic acid in a test tube. Add a few drops of potassium manganate(VII) solution and warm gently.

24 Are there any signs of reaction?

25 Is ethanoic acid easily oxidised?

CORROSIVE
Concentrated sulphuric acid
Concentrated ethanoic acid

Experiment 7:
Dehydration

Put 2 cm³ of concentrated sulphuric acid in a boiling tube and warm it **gently (CARE)**. Now add a few drops of concentrated ethanoic acid to the warm sulphuric acid and observe carefully to see if any gas is evolved. If a gas comes off, attempt to identify it.

26 Is ethanoic acid readily dehydrated by concentrated sulphuric acid?

The reactions of ethanoic acid that you have seen in the first part of the practical are typical of carboxylic acids in general. Methanoic acid and ethanedioic acid are not typical, however, and you will now look at some of their properties.

(2) Some properties of methanoic acid

> **CARE!**
> *Methanoic acid is corrosive and its vapour is irritant. Eye protection must be worn.*

CORROSIVE
Methanoic acid

**EYE PROTECTION
MUST BE WORN**

Experiment 8:
Physical properties

Investigate the smell (**CARE**) and the solubility in water of methanoic acid.

27 Are these properties similar to those of ethanoic acid?

HIGHLY FLAMMABLE
Ethanol

Experiment 9:
Esterification

Repeat the esterification experiment, as in experiment 5, using ethanol instead of pentanol and methanoic acid instead of ethanoic acid.

28 Describe the smell of the vapour.

29 Name and write the structural formula of the ester that has been formed.

30 Does methanoic acid behave in a similar way to ethanoic acid in this reaction?

Experiment 10:
Oxidation

Repeat the oxidation experiment, as in experiment 6, using methanoic acid instead of ethanoic acid.

31 Are there signs of reaction?

32 Is methanoic acid easily oxidised? If so, to what?

Experiment 11:
Dehydration

Repeat the dehydration experiment, as in experiment 7, using methanoic acid instead of ethanoic acid.

33 Is methanoic acid readily dehydrated? If so, what is formed?

(3) Some properties of ethanedioic acid

Experiment 12:
Physical properties

Investigate the smell and the solubility in water of ethanedioic acid.

34 Compare the volatility of ethanedioic acid with that of methanoic and ethanoic acids.

35 Relate any difference in volatility to the structure of ethanedioic acid.

36 Compare the solubility of ethanedioic acid with that of the other two acids. Attempt to explain any differences.

Experiment 13:
Esterification

Repeat the esterification experiment as in experiment 5, using ethanol instead of pentanol and ethanedioic acid instead of ethanoic acid.

37 Describe the smell of the vapour.

38 Name and write the structural formula of the ester that has been formed.

39 Is the volatility of this ester similar to the volatility of the ethanoate and methanoate esters you prepared?

40 Explain your answer to question 39 in view of the difference in volatility between ethanedioic acid and the other two acids.

Experiment 14:
Oxidation

Repeat the oxidation experiment, as in experiment 6, using an aqueous solution of ethanedioic acid instead of ethanoic acid.

41 Are there signs of reaction?

42 Is ethanedioic acid easily oxidised? If so, to what?

CARE!
Ethanedioic acid is harmful and irritant.

IRRITANT
Ethanedioic acid

**EYE PROTECTION
MUST BE WORN**

HARMFUL
Ethanedioic acid

HIGHLY FLAMMABLE
Ethanol

Experiment 15:
Dehydration

Repeat the dehydration experiment, as in experiment 7, using ethanedioic acid instead of ethanoic acid.

43 Is ethanedioic acid readily dehydrated? If so, what is formed?

44 Draw up a table summarising the reactions of carboxylic acids and showing the results for each of the three acids in this practical.

Investigation

See Investigation S1

Practical 34

Amines

REQUIREMENTS

Each student, or pair of students, will need:

Eye protection

Rack with 4 test tubes

Teat pipette

2 small beakers (100 cm³)

Universal indicator paper

Boiling tube

Thermometer (0 °C–110 °C)

Butylamine (**highly flammable** and **corrosive**)

Phenylamine (**toxic**)

Ethanoyl chloride (acetyl chloride) (**highly flammable** and **corrosive**)

Benzoyl chloride (**corrosive**)

Ammonium chloride (**harmful**)

Sodium nitrite (**oxidising** and **toxic**)

Concentrated hydrochloric acid (**corrosive**)

Phenol (**toxic** and **corrosive**)

2-Naphthol (**very toxic** and **corrosive**)

Bromine water (**toxic** and **corrosive**)

Ice

Ammonia (**irritant**)

Hydrochloric acid (**irritant**)

Sodium hydroxide (**corrosive**)

Copper(II) sulphate solution (about 0.1 mol dm⁻³)

Access to a fume cupboard

Time required 2½ hours

WEAR PROTECTIVE GLOVES

USE A FUME CUPBOARD

TOXIC Phenylamine

HIGHLY FLAMMABLE Butylamine

IRRITANT Butylamine

CORROSIVE Butylamine

Introduction

Amines are one of the most important groups of organic compounds containing nitrogen. They can be regarded as derivatives of ammonia in which one or more of the hydrogen atoms in NH_3 is replaced by aryl or alkyl groups. If only one of the hydrogen atoms in NH_3 is substituted, we get a compound of the form RNH_2, called a primary amine. The simplest primary amines are CH_3NH_2, methylamine, and $CH_3CH_2NH_2$, ethylamine.

> 1 Write full structural formulae for ammonia, butylamine and phenylamine (aniline).
>
> 2 Which simple substance would you expect amines to resemble?
>
> 3 Predict two properties of butylamine.

Free amines are relatively rare in nature, but they do occur in decomposing protein such as meat and fish. Normally the $-NH_2$ group is associated with other functional groups, as in amino acids, for example. Compounds containing the $-NH_2$ group are important in the manufacture of drugs, dyes and nylon.

In this practical you will consider the properties of an alkylamine (butylamine) and an arylamine (phenylamine) and compare their properties with those of ammonia. Butylamine is chosen because it is a liquid and not too volatile. Phenylamine is also a liquid, colourless when pure, but the sample you use is likely to be dark-coloured due to atmospheric oxidation.

> **CARE!**
> *Eye protection must be worn throughout this practical.*

EYE PROTECTION MUST BE WORN

A   Reactions of amines as bases

> **CARE!**
> *Phenylamine is toxic and harmful by skin absorption. Avoid all skin contact. Wear protective gloves and work in a fume cupboard.*
> *Butylamine is flammable and an irritant.*

(1) Reaction with water and indicators

Shake 2 drops of butylamine and 2 drops of phenylamine separately with 2 cm³ of water. Now test each of these solutions and a solution of ammonia with universal indicator paper.

> 4 Comment on the solubility of the amines in water and account for any differences in solubility.
>
> 5 Comment on the basic strength of the amines relative to ammonia and account for any differences in their strength as bases.

(2) Reaction with dilute hydrochloric acid

CORROSIVE
Sodium hydroxide
solution

IRRITANT
Dilute hydrochloric
acid

Shake 2 drops of butylamine and 2 drops of phenylamine separately with 2 cm³ of dilute hydrochloric acid.

> 6 Describe what happens.
>
> 7 Write equations for the reactions which have occurred.
>
> 8 Explain the differing solubility of phenylamine in water and in dilute hydrochloric acid.

Add dilute sodium hydroxide solution to the solution of phenylamine in hydrochloric acid until the mixture is alkaline.

> 9 Describe and explain what happens.

B Reactions of amines as ligands

Reaction with copper(II) sulphate solution

Add ammonia solution drop by drop to 2 cm³ of copper(II) sulphate solution until the ammonia is present in excess.

> 10 Describe and explain what happens. Write equations for the reactions which occur.

Repeat the experiment using first butylamine and then phenylamine in place of ammonia solution.

> 11 Describe and explain what happens. Do the amines react in a similar way to ammonia?

**EYE PROTECTION
MUST BE WORN**

**USE A FUME
CUPBOARD**

HIGHLY FLAMMABLE
Ethanoyl chloride

CORROSIVE
Ethanoyl chloride
Benzoyl chloride

C Reactions of amines as nucleophiles

(1) Reaction with ethanoyl chloride and benzoyl chloride

CARE!
Work in a fume cupboard. Eye protection must be worn.

Ammonia and amines can act as nucleophiles in attacking the positive centres in molecules such as ethanoyl chloride, CH_3COCl, and benzoyl chloride, C_6H_5COCl. For example, ammonia reacts very vigorously with ethanoyl chloride, forming ethanamide.

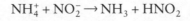

12 Would you expect phenylamine to react with ethanoyl chloride more or less vigorously than ammonia reacts? Explain your answer.

Put 1 cm³ of phenylamine in a boiling tube. **Carefully** add 1 cm³ of ethanoyl chloride drop by drop, shaking after the addition of each drop.

13 Describe what happens.

14 Write an equation for the reaction which occurs. Name the solid organic product.

(2) Reaction with nitrous acid

HARMFUL
Ammonium chloride

Dissolve a full spatula measure of ammonium chloride in 3 cm³ of hot water. Now add a spatula measure of solid sodium nitrite.

The reaction can be regarded as a reaction between ammonia and nitrous acid, these two substances being formed from ammonium ions and nitrite ions:

$$NH_4^+ + NO_2^- \rightarrow NH_3 + HNO_2$$

CORROSIVE
Concentrated
hydrochloric acid
Butylamine

OXIDISING
Sodium nitrite

TOXIC
Sodium nitrite
Phenylamine

15 Describe and explain what happens.

Put three drops of butylamine in a test tube and add concentrated hydrochloric acid drop by drop until a clear solution is formed. Dilute the mixture to 3 cm³ with water, add a spatula measure of sodium nitrite and warm gently. Repeat the experiment using phenylamine in place of butylamine.

The reaction can be regarded as a reaction between the amine and nitrous acid, HNO_2.

**HIGHLY
FLAMMABLE**
Butylamine

16 Describe and explain what happens. Write equations for the reactions which occur.

Amines react with nitrous acid to form diazonium compounds:

$$RNH_2 + HNO_2 \rightarrow R-\overset{+}{N}\equiv N + {}^-OH + H_2O$$
$$\text{diazonium ion}$$

Unless the diazonium ion is stabilised in some way, it decomposes forming nitrogen and the new carbocation R^+, which takes part in a variety of further reactions.

$$R—\overset{+}{N}\equiv N \rightarrow R^+ + N_2$$

In the case of arylamines, such as $C_6H_5NH_2$, the diazonium ion is stabilised by delocalisation of electrons from the benzene ring. The diazonium compound is stable provided the temperature of the reactants is kept below 10 °C. These diazonium compounds are useful reactive intermediates, as the following experiment shows.

Make a solution of 2 drops of phenylamine in 2 cm³ of dilute hydrochloric acid and add it to about 5 cm³ of a crushed ice/water mixture at 5 °C – 10 °C. Add to this mixture a spatula measure of sodium nitrite and stir well to ensure that the solid dissolves. This solution contains the benzenediazonium ion, $C_6H_5—\overset{+}{N}\equiv N$.

Use the solution to prepare azo dyes as follows.

> **CARE!**
> *Phenol is toxic. Avoid skin contact and wear gloves and eye protection in experiment A which follows.*

CORROSIVE
Phenol

WEAR PROTECTIVE GLOVES

A Dissolve a spatula measure of phenol in 2 cm³ of dilute sodium hydroxide solution. Cool this solution to below 5 °C and add the diazonium solution drop by drop.

B Repeat the test using 2-naphthol in place of phenol.

EYE PROTECTION MUST BE WORN

HARMFUL
2-naphthol

> **17** Describe what happens in each case. Write equations for the reactions which occur. (See *Chemistry in Context*, Fifth Edition, section 33.7.)
>
> **18** Why is it so important to keep the solutions below 10 °C in these reactions?

D Reactions of the aromatic ring in phenylamine

Put 3 drops of phenylamine in a test tube and add concentrated hydrochloric acid (**CARE**) drop by drop until the phenylamine dissolves. Now add bromine water drop by drop until no further change occurs.

CORROSIVE
Concentrated hydrochloric acid
Bromine water

VERY TOXIC
Bromine water

EYE PROTECTION MUST BE WORN

> **19** Describe what happens. Write an equation for the reaction.
>
> **20** Why can phenylamine undergo substitution with bromine so much more easily than benzene?

Practical 35

Polymers

REQUIREMENTS

Each student, or pair of students, will require:

Eye protection

Rack and 4 test tubes

2 boiling tubes

Beaker (400 cm^3)

Beaker (100 cm^3)

Glass rod

Tweezers

2 disposable polystyrene cups (normal, not expanded polystyrene)

Cotton wool

Broken porcelain

Tongs

Sharp knife or scissors

Access to a fume cupboard

Access to an oven

Phenylethene (styrene) (**harmful** and **flammable**: should be fresh)

Di(dodecanoyl)peroxide (lauroyl peroxide: **oxidising** and **irritant**)

5% solution (freshly prepared) of decanedioyl dichloride (sebacoyl chloride: **corrosive**) in cyclohexane (**highly flammable** and **harmful**) (10 cm^3) (**irritant**)

5% solution of 1,6-diaminohexane in water (10 cm^3) (**irritant**)

Concentrated sulphuric acid (**very corrosive**)

40% aqueous solution of methanal (formalin: **toxic** and **corrosive**)

Urea

Polystyrene chips, or fragments of a polystyrene cup, toy etc.

Natural rubber, small pieces

Urea–methanal plastic, small pieces (pieces of a broken white electrical fitting such as a plug or a socket would do)

Methylbenzene (**harmful** and **highly flammable**)

Samples of polythene film, high and low density. To make comparison easier, the samples need to be of similar thickness. For example:

- low density: polythene sheeting from a garden centre or hardware store
- high density: cut from food containers such as large plastic milk bottles

Time required $2\frac{1}{2}$–4 hours

Introduction

This practical is in two parts. In the first part you will prepare some representative polymers. In the second part you will investigate the way in which the molecular structure of a polymer can influence its physical properties. You may find it helpful to refer to *Chemistry in Context*, Fifth Edition, Sections 27.7, 27.8 and 27.9, during this practical and in answering the questions.

A   The preparation of some polymers

Polymers can be classified in a number of ways. One way is to group them according to the type of chemical reaction by which they are prepared. Thus, there are **addition polymers** and **condensation polymers**.

> **1**   Explain the terms 'addition' and 'condensation' as applied to chemical reactions.

Polymers differ in the way in which they behave when heated. **Thermoplastic** materials soften on heating and harden again on cooling. **Thermosetting** materials set hard on heating and cannot be softened or melted. Strong heating decomposes them.

> **2**   Name one article made from a thermoplastic material and one made from a thermosetting material.

The strength and elasticity of polymers varies widely. Highly elastic polymers are called **elastomers**. **Fibres** have low elasticity and high tensile strength. Intermediate between elastomers and fibres are **plastics**.

> **3**   Name one elastomer, one plastic and one fibre.

> **CARE!**
> *Eye protection must be worn throughout this practical.*

EYE PROTECTION MUST BE WORN

The preparation of an addition polymer: polystyrene

Polystyrene, systematically called poly(phenylethene), is made by polymerising phenylethene (styrene), whose formula is shown. A

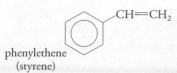

phenylethene
(styrene)

catalyst di(dodecanoyl) peroxide (lauroyl peroxide) is needed to speed up the polymerisation, which is otherwise very slow.

Working in a fume cupboard, put 10 cm^3 of phenylethene in a boiling tube. Add about 0.2 g of di(dodecanoyl) peroxide and shake the tube until the catalyst has dissolved. Plug the tube with cotton wool and heat it in a water bath at about 100 °C for 20 minutes. Now examine the contents and compare with the original phenylethene.

USE A FUME CUPBOARD

EYE PROTECTION MUST BE WORN

> **4** What evidence is there that polymerisation is taking place?
>
> **5** Draw the structure of a section of the polymer chain.

IRRITANT
Phenylethene
Di(dodecanoyl)
peroxide

OXIDISING
Di(dodecanoyl)peroxide

FLAMMABLE
Phenylethene

Polymerisation can be completed by heating the tube in an oven or water bath at about 50 °C until a solid block is obtained. Of course, the glass tube would have to be broken to remove the polymer. Alternatively, the semi-polymerised material can be used as a casting or embedding resin by pouring it into a mould which has been lightly smeared with liquid detergent.

> **6** Classify polystyrene as:
>
> **a** thermoplastic or thermosetting,
> **b** elastomer, plastic or fibre.

The preparation of a condensation polymer – nylon 6,10

Nylon 6,10 is prepared by a condensation reaction between decanedioyl dichloride (sebacoyl chloride) and 1,6-diaminohexane.

$$\text{Cl} \quad \text{C} - CH_2CH_2CH_2CH_2CH_2CH_2CH_2CH_2 - \text{C} \quad \text{Cl}$$
$$\text{O} \qquad\qquad\qquad\qquad\qquad\qquad\qquad\qquad \text{O}$$

decanedioyl dichloride

$$H_2NCH_2CH_2CH_2CH_2CH_2CH_2NH_2$$

1,6-diaminohexane

Work in a fume cupboard. Put 10 cm^3 of a 5% solution of 1,6-diaminohexane in water into a 100 cm^3 beaker.

EYE PROTECTION MUST BE WORN

USE A FUME CUPBOARD

CORROSIVE
Decanedioyl
dichloride

IRRITANT
1,6-Diaminohexane in water

HIGHLY FLAMMABLE
Decanedioyl chloride in cyclohexane

> **CARE!**
> *The vapour from this solution is harmful.*

Very carefully, using a dropping pipette, add 10 cm^3 of a 5% solution of decanedioyl dichloride in cyclohexane. Do **not** allow the two solutions to mix – try to float one layer on top of the other so that the nylon forms at the interface. Use tweezers to pull the interface film out of the liquid and wind it on to a glass rod. The glass rod can then be rotated, pulling a continuous filament of nylon from the interface and winding it on to the rod (figure 1). **Do not touch this filament by hand, even after washing it.**

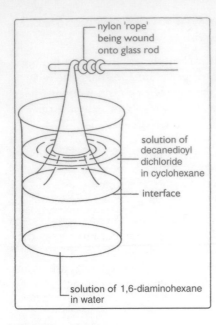

Figure 1
The nylon rope trick.

7 Draw the structure of a section of the nylon 6,10 chain.

8 What other product is formed in this reaction, apart from nylon?

9 What reagents would you use if you were making nylon 6,6?

10 Classify nylon as:

  a thermoplastic or thermosetting,
  b elastomer, plastic or fibre.

The preparation of a thermosetting plastic: urea–methanal resin

Urea and methanal react together to form a polymer chain as shown in figure 2. These chains can then cross-link with other chains via further molecules of methanal (figure 3). The extensive cross-linking in this polymer makes it set hard on formation and prevents it from softening on heating. (See part B of this practical).

$$H_2N-\overset{\overset{\displaystyle O}{\|}}{C}-NH_2 \quad + \quad \overset{\displaystyle H \quad H}{\underset{\overset{\|}{O}}{C}} \quad + \quad H_2N-\overset{\overset{\displaystyle O}{\|}}{C}-NH_2 \quad + \quad \overset{\displaystyle H \quad H}{\underset{\overset{\|}{O}}{C}}$$

urea   methanal

$$H_2N-\overset{\overset{\displaystyle O}{\|}}{C}-NH-\overset{\overset{\displaystyle H}{|}}{\underset{\underset{\displaystyle H}{|}}{C}}-HN-\overset{\overset{\displaystyle O}{\|}}{C}-NH-\overset{\overset{\displaystyle H}{|}}{\underset{\underset{\displaystyle H}{|}}{C}}-$$

$$+ H_2O \qquad\qquad + H_2O$$

Figure 2
Polymerisation of urea and methanal.

$$-NH-\overset{\overset{\displaystyle O}{\|}}{C}-NH-CH_2-NH-\overset{\overset{\displaystyle O}{\|}}{C}-NH-CH_2-$$

$$H_2C=O \qquad\qquad H_2C=O$$

$$-NH-\overset{\overset{\displaystyle O}{\|}}{C}-NH-CH_2-NH-\overset{\overset{\displaystyle O}{\|}}{C}-NH-CH_2-$$

$$-NH-\overset{\overset{\displaystyle O}{\|}}{C}-\overset{\overset{\displaystyle CH_2}{|}}{N}-CH_2-NH-\overset{\overset{\displaystyle O}{\|}}{C}-\overset{\overset{\displaystyle CH_2}{|}}{N}-CH_2-$$

$$-NH-\overset{\overset{\displaystyle O}{\|}}{C}-N-CH_2-NH-\overset{\overset{\displaystyle O}{\|}}{C}-N-CH_2-$$

$$+H_2O \qquad\qquad +H_2O$$

Figure 3
Cross-linking between urea–methanal chains.

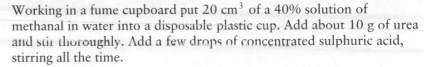
CARE!
Methanol has toxic and corrosive vapour.

USE A FUME CUPBOARD

EYE PROTECTION MUST BE WORN

TOXIC
Methanal

VERY CORROSIVE
Concentrated
sulphuric acid
Methanal

Working in a fume cupboard put 20 cm³ of a 40% solution of methanal in water into a disposable plastic cup. Add about 10 g of urea and stir thoroughly. Add a few drops of concentrated sulphuric acid, stirring all the time.

When polymerisation is complete, it should be possible to remove the solid mass of polymer intact from the container. Wash the polymer thoroughly before handling.

11 Describe the appearance of the polymer.

12 Is this a condensation polymer or an addition polymer?

13 What was the purpose of the concentrated sulphuric acid?

14 This polymer is often used to make electrical fittings such as plugs. How could this polymer be made into the shape of an electrical plug, bearing in mind that it is a thermosetting material?

B   The properties of some polymers

The properties of polymers can be related to their molecular structure. A number of molecular properties are particularly important in deciding the strength, elasticity, solubility and softening point of polymers.

(1) Chain length

In general, increasing the chain length increases the strength of a polymer.

(2) Cross-linking

A high degree of cross-linking reduces the extent to which the individual chains can move. This reduces elasticity and increases hardness and softening point (figure 4).

(3) Crystallinity

No polymer is completely crystalline – in some regions the chains are regularly arranged and in others they are at random (figure 5). A polymer will therefore have both crystalline and amorphous (non-crystalline) regions, although the proportion of one to the other will vary according to the polymer. A high degree of crystallinity increases the density, the softening point and the tensile strength of the polymer. Crystalline polymers are usually opaque, while non-crystalline ones are usually transparent and glassy. Fibres have very high crystallinity, but in elastomers crystallinity is very low.

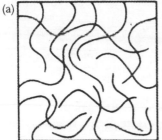

(a)

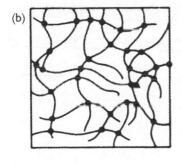

(b)

Figure 4
a Polymer with no cross-linking.
b Polymer with high degree of cross-linking.

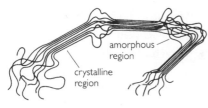

amorphous region

crystalline region

Figure 5
Crystalline and amorphous regions in a polymer.

Two factors are of major importance in determining the degree of crystallinity.

i Intermolecular forces between chains

A polymer carrying highly polar groups along its chain will have strong interactions between chains and this will tend to increase crystallinity.

ii Shape of the chains

Linear chains pack together well, giving high crystallinity. Chains carrying many branches, or with irregularly arranged side-groups, pack together less well, giving lower crystallinity.

Experiment 1: Effect of cross-linking on properties

In these tests, polystyrene will be used as an example of a linear polymer with no cross-linking, urea–methanal resin as an example of a highly cross-linked polymer, and vulcanised natural rubber as an example of a polymer with an intermediate degree of cross-linking.

CARE!
Molten plastics can cause severe burns, and the fumes from burning plastics are often toxic.

Working in a fume cupboard, gently heat a small sample of each polymer in turn on a piece of broken porcelain.

> **15** Compare the effect of heating the three polymers, and relate it to the degree of cross-linking in the material. Bear in mind that the polymers may contain additives such as dyes or filters, which may modify their properties.

Investigate the effect of methylbenzene, an aromatic hydrocarbon solvent, on each polymer in turn.

Look for signs of the polymer dissolving, softening or swelling.

> **16** Tabulate your results and try to explain them in terms of the nature of the solvent used and the degree of cross-linking in the polymer.

CORROSIVE
Fumes from burning plastics

TOXIC
Fumes from burning plastics

USE A FUME CUPBOARD

HARMFUL
Methylbenzene

EYE PROTECTION MUST BE WORN

HIGHLY FLAMMABLE
Methylbenzene

Experiment 2: The effect of 'cold drawing' on the crystallinity of a polymer: the effect of stretching polythene film

With a sharp pair of scissors or a sharp knife cut out a strip of low-density polythene film about 10 cm long and 2 cm wide. Make sure the edges of the strip are clean-cut. Stretch the film lengthways by pulling it slowly and steadily – avoid sudden jerks. Record any changes that occur in the film as you stretch. Note any changes in the width of the strip, its

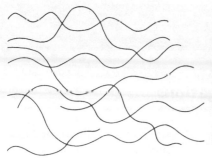

Figure 6
Polythene chains before cold drawing.

appearance, its elasticity and its strength, as indicated by the force required to stretch it.

17 What changes occur in the crystallinity of the polythene as it is stretched?

18 If the polymer chains are distributed as shown in figure 6 before stretching, indicate by a sketch how you think they may be arranged after stretching.

19 The operation you have just carried out is called 'cold drawing'. What industrial importance does this process have?

Repeat the experiment using a fresh strip of polythene, but this time stop pulling when you think the crystallinity of the sample has reached a maximum, but before it breaks. Now pull the strip across its width, that is at right angles to the original direction of stretching.

20 What happens? Suggest an explanation in terms of the arrangement of the polymer chains.

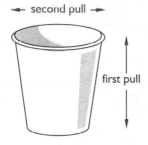

Figure 7
Tearing a polystyrene cup.

Take a polystyrene drinking cup (made of normal, not expanded polystyrene) and try to tear it, pulling in the first direction shown in figure 7.

Now try to tear it at right angles, pulling in the second direction shown in figure 7.

21 Suggest a reason for any differences in the ease with which the polystyrene can be torn in the different directions.

Experiment 3:
Comparing low- and high-density polythene

Low-density polythene contains chains which are branched. In high-density polythene the chains are unbranched. This means the chains can pack more closely together.

22 Use samples of high-density and low-density polythene film to compare the following properties:

 – transparency,
 – flexibility,
 – softening in hot water,
 – texture,
 – density.

23 Try to relate the differences in properties to the different structures of the two forms.

Investigations

Some general guidance on Investigations

In an Investigation you have more control over what you do than in ordinary practical work. You are expected to plan and make decisions for yourself. This means that Investigations usually take longer than the kind of practical work where you follow instructions, but they are often more enjoyable because you are in control.

Finding references

The Investigations in this book have been divided into **Shorter Investigations**, requiring about 3–4 hours of experimental work, and **Longer Investigations**, requiring about 10 – 12 hours. Each Investigation gives enough information to start you off, but leaves a lot for you to do yourself. You will need to find references to help you with the design of your Investigation, and to give you the chemical background. You may need to refer to your teacher for help with suggested references. Be sure to list all the references you use at the end of your report.

Planning your Investigation

You must have a clear plan of action before you start. Among other things, you will need to decide the following.

- What exactly are you going to investigate? The Investigations in this book are a starting point, but you will need to formulate the particular aspects you are going to investigate. It is always best to put the title of your Investigation in the form of a question, for example: 'What affects the activity of an enzyme?'
- What chemicals will you use? You will need to consider what is available, and what is safe to use.
- What apparatus will you use? Again, you will need to consider what is available.
- What are the health and safety considerations? (See the next section entitled 'Checking health and safety'.)
- What observations and measurements will you make?
- How will you control variables? For example, if you are investigating the rate of a reaction which is affected by both temperature and pH, you will need to think about how you will keep the temperature constant while you vary pH, and vice versa.

You may find that you need to modify your plans as you go along. Nevertheless, it is important to make careful plans before you start.

You MUST check your plans with your teacher before starting any practical work.

Checking health and safety

(See also 'Safety in the Chemistry Laboratory', pages ix–xi)
Your teacher will need to approve your plans from the point of view of health and safety, but it will help if you carry out your own risk assessment.

A risk assessment identifies all the hazards associated with the chemicals you will be using, and those you will be making. It also gives ways to reduce the risks from these hazards and lists the control measures that need to be taken.

The stages in carrying out a risk assessment

1 List all the chemicals you will be using, and those you will be making. Give the form in which they will be used and the quantities. For solutions, give the concentration you will be using.

Chemistry in Context Laboratory Manual

2 Identify any hazard associated with each substance listed in **1**. The types of hazards you are likely to meet are listed in table 1 on page ix. Your teacher will advise you on where to look up the hazards. If you refer to older publications, remember that safety standards may have changed.

3 Now consider the *operations* you will be carrying out with the chemicals. What are the hazards associated with these operations? (For example, heating certain substances can give rise to a fire hazard; or you might estimate the likely concentration of hazardous gases and thus decide if you need to use the fume cupboard.)

4 Consider whether replacing a hazardous chemical by a less hazardous one (including a lower concentration) would reduce the risk.

5 Finally, list all the safety precautions that you will need to take in view of the hazards you have identified in points **2** and **3**.

Include the risk assessment in your plans for the Investigation. Discuss it with your teacher before you start any work. Remember – if you change your plans, you may have to change your risk assessment.

Carrying out your Investigation

It is important to record all your results as you go along. You never know which may prove useful later!

Don't worry too much if you seem to be getting unexpected results. Many important scientific discoveries were made when scientists obtained unexpected results. If things really do seem to be going wrong, you may need to change your plans – but remember to consider the health and safety implications and to discuss any changes with your teacher.

Writing up a report on your Investigation

Your teacher will advise you on how the Investigation should be written up.

A good report will include:
- a clear description of what you were investigating,
- a risk assessment with a clear statement of any safety precautions,
- a description of what you did. This should include:
  - the principle behind your method
  - the variables you measured, and those you controlled
  - the apparatus you used, including diagrams where appropriate
  - the chemicals you used, including quantities and concentrations where appropriate
  - details of any trial experiments you carried out,
- a list of the precautions which you took to obtain more accurate and more reliable results,
- any difficulties you encountered, and any changes you made to your approach,
- *all* your results and calculations,
- tables, graphs and diagrams wherever they are appropriate,
- your conclusions,
- an assessment of errors, if your investigation was a quantitative one, and a comment on the accuracy of your results compared with accepted (data book) values,
- suggestions for how your method could be improved,
- a list of references consulted.

Investigations

Shorter Investigations

S1 How acidic is vinegar?

The main component of household vinegar is ethanoic acid. Investigate the concentration of the acid in white vinegar by titrating it against a solution of sodium hydroxide.

You will probably need to do a preliminary experiment to find out the approximate concentration of sodium hydroxide solution to use in your titration. You will also need to select a suitable indicator.

You can extend your investigation to find the concentration of ethanoic acid in other types of

vinegar that are available in the supermarket. If the vinegar is coloured, you will have to devise a way to remove the colour before adding the indicator. Alternatively, you could use a different technique for finding the end-point of your titration.

In reality, ethanoic acid is not the only acidic substance in vinegar. How could you separate the ethanoic acid from other acids present? If you have time, plan and carry out a scheme to extend your investigation in this way.

relates to
Practicals 7 and 33

Before you start, you must:
- carry out a risk assessment,
- discuss your plans with your teacher.

S2 Designing a thermochemical titration

Enthalpy changes of neutralisation can be used to find the concentration of a solution of an acid or alkali. The idea is similar to the titration of an acid with an alkali using an indicator. Instead of observing the colour change of an indicator, in thermochemical titrations the temperature change is measured as the acid reacts with the alkali.

Design a method for carrying out a thermochemical titration. Try it out, and compare its accuracy with a

conventional titration using an indicator. Try to improve the accuracy of your method.

There is an opportunity to use datalogging if you have a suitable computer, interface and probe available.

When might this type of titration be particularly useful?

relates to
Practical 7

Before you start, you must:
- carry out a risk assessment,
- discuss your plans with your teacher.

Chemistry in Context Laboratory Manual

S3 Designing a conductivity titration

You can find the concentration of an acid or alkali by measuring changes in conductivity during neutralisation. The idea is similar to the titration of an acid with an alkali using an indicator. Instead of observing the colour change of an indicator, the conductivity of the solution is measured as the acid reacts with the alkali.

Design a method for carrying out a conductivity titration. Try it out and compare its accuracy with a conventional titration using an indicator. Try using both strong and weak acids and alkalis.

This is a good opportunity to use datalogging if you have a computer, interface and probe available.

When might this type of titration be particularly useful?

Investigation

relates to
Practical 7

> Before you start, you must:
> - carry out a risk assessment,
> - discuss your plans with your teacher.

S4 Investigating the effect of a charged rod on liquid jets

You have probably found that a charged rod causes a jet of liquid to deflect. Polar liquids such as water tend to be deflected more than non-polar liquids such as hexane.

The explanation for this behaviour is that polar molecules become lined up as the liquid flows past the rod. The charge at one end of the molecules lines up with the opposite charge on the rod. The attraction between the opposite charges causes the jet to deflect.

However, *non-polar* liquids are also attracted to a charged rod to some extent, because the rod induces temporary dipoles in the molecules.

Investigation

relates to
Practical 6

Investigate the factors which determine how much a liquid jet is deflected. For example, you might investigate:

- the effect of changing the polarity of the liquid – for example, you might investigate different members of the homologous series of alcohols,
- the effect of mixing a polar liquid with a non-polar one,
- the extent to which the density of a liquid affects its deflection.

In making a risk assessment, you will need to bear in mind that some of the solvents you use may be hazardous in some way. It will be necessary to work in a fume cupboard.

> Before you start, you must:
> - carry out a risk assessment,
> - discuss your plans with your teacher.

S5 Using enthalpy changes for cooling

Campers and others without access to a refrigerator can keep food and drinks cool by lowering the temperature of an insulated container using chemical means.

A convenient method is to add a salt with an endothermic enthalpy change of solution to water in a plastic bag within the insulated container.

Devise a system that could be used to keep food cool. Here are some points which you might like to think about.

- What salts can be used? Cost, safety and availability need to be borne in mind, as well as suitability of enthalpy change of solution.

- What temperature drop is required?

- What quantities of salt and water are needed to achieve the required temperature drop?

- Does the system work in practice?

Investigation
relates to
Practical 9

Before you start, you must:
- carry out a risk assessment,
- discuss your plans with your teacher.

S6 Concentration cells

Figure 2 in Practical 11 shows an example of a concentration cell. Investigate this and other concentration cells. You might investigate:

- the maximum voltage obtainable,

- the mathematical relationship between the concentrations in the two half-cells and the overall cell voltage,

- whether the same relationship applies for cells based on other half-cells besides $Cu(s)/Cu^{2+}(aq)$. Another half-cell that you could investigate is $Fe(s)/Fe^{2+}(aq)$.

Investigation
relates to
Practical 11

Before you start, you must:
- carry out a risk assessment,
- discuss your plans with your teacher.

S7 Studying the kinetics of reactions between metals and acids

How will the reaction of magnesium with dilute sulphuric acid compare with the reactions of zinc or iron?

How will the reaction of zinc with dilute sulphuric acid compare with its reaction with dilute hydrochloric acid?

The equations for the reactions of these metals with acids are very similar, but are the kinetic features also similar?

The quantities which best describe the kinetic features of a reaction are its rate equation and its activation energy.

Neither the rate equation nor the activation energy can be obtained from the balanced chemical equation. The rate equation can be obtained by studying the reaction rate at different concentrations. The activation energy can be obtained by studying the reaction rate at different temperatures.

Decide which reactions and which kinetic features you are going to study. You will then need to decide:

- how you will obtain a measure of reaction rate,
- the quantities you will use,
- how you will obtain the kinetic features (the rate equation and/or the activation energy) from the results of your experiments.

Before you start, you must:
- carry out a risk assessment,
- discuss your plans with your teacher.

S8 How fast does carbon dioxide escape from solution?

Fizzy drinks go 'flat' as the dissolved carbon dioxide escapes from solution. Investigate the factors affecting the rate at which the carbon dioxide escapes.

It is easier to follow the changes in concentration of carbon dioxide in the aqueous rather than the gas phase. You can do this indirectly by measuring the pH of the solution. In solution, a small amount of carbon dioxide reacts with water to form a weakly acidic solution.

$$CO_2(aq) + H_2O(l) \rightarrow HCO_3^-(aq) + H^+(aq)$$

A saturated solution of carbon dioxide has a pH of 3.9 at room temperature and pressure, compared with 7.0 for pure water.

The pH of the solution thus gives an indirect measure of the concentration of CO_2 in solution: it is a rough measure only, but good enough for the kind of comparisons you will be making. pH is a logarithmic scale, and if the concentration of CO_2 is halved, the pH rises by only 0.3. The pH changes you observe will therefore be small, and you will need to design your investigation to give the largest changes possible. If a computer interface and pH probe are available, you could use them to monitor the pH changes.

Begin by listing all the factors that you think will affect the rate at which CO_2 comes off, then decide which a particular factor(s) you will investigate.

Before you start, you must:
- carry out a risk assessment,
- discuss your plans with your teacher.

Investigations

S9 Investigating the activity of an enzyme

Diabetes can be detected by testing for glucose in a patient's urine.

A test that is often used involves test strips which contain the enzyme glucose oxidase. This enzyme oxidises glucose to gluconic acid and hydrogen peroxide.

The test strips also contain a redox indicator, whose colour changes to blue when it is oxidised by hydrogen peroxide. The test strips thus provide a quick and simple test for glucose of the concentration typically found in the urine of

diabetics. This concentration is about 0.02 mol dm^{-3}. They also provide you with a handy way of testing the activity of the enzyme glucose oxidase.

Investigate factors affecting the activity of glucose oxidase. You might investigate one or more of the following factors:

- specificity: the normal substrate for this enzyme is glucose, but does it work with other sugars?

- temperature,

- pH.

There are several brands of test strips. If necessary, ask your teacher for information about how to get them. Make sure you read the instructions on the packet.

Before you start, you must:
- carry out a risk assessment,
- discuss your plans with your teacher.

S10 Investigating sunscreens

The Sun's radiation includes ultraviolet rays, which can damage the skin and sometimes cause skin cancer. Sunscreens protect the skin by absorbing ultraviolet radiation, especially the higher energy radiations, which are particularly damaging.

Sunscreens can be bought as lotions which are applied to the skin. There are in fact many chemical substances which absorb ultraviolet, including glass, which explains why people do not get sunburnt when sitting behind a window on a sunny day.

Investigate the effectiveness of different substances as sunscreens. You could look at commercial sunscreen lotions, but also other materials that are relevant, such as glass, water and Perspex.

You will need a source of ultraviolet radiation, and a method for detecting it. The best source is the Sun. However, this may not always be practical, and you may need to use some kind of ultraviolet lamp. If you do, be sure to follow the safety instructions since some ultraviolet lamps can burn the skin and permanently damage the eyes.

There are several ways in which you could detect ultraviolet radiation.

1 Ultraviolet-sensitive paper, which turns blue when exposed to ultraviolet from the Sun. Your teacher will be able to tell you if this is available.

2 Most machine washing powders contain fluorescers. A piece of white cloth washed in such powder will give a bright fluorescent glow under ultraviolet radiation.

3 Some brands of photocopying paper fluoresce under ultraviolet radiation.

Before you start, you must:
- carry out a risk assessment,
- discuss your plans with your teacher.

S11 The formula of the aspirin/copper(II) complex

Aspirin (2-ethanoylhydroxybenzoic acid) has been used for a long time to relieve pain and control inflammation. In some cases gram quantities are needed, which can have adverse side effects. Copper complexes of anti-inflammatory medicines have been found to be more effective and involve fewer side effects than the original drug.

Experiment 1 in Practical 13 gives a method for finding the formula of a complex ion using colorimetry. *You can use this method to investigate the formula of the complex formed between copper(II) ions and aspirin.*

You will need to convert your aspirin into its salt by reaction with potassium hydrogencarbonate solution. Design, and then carry out, a procedure using a solution of the aspirin salt and a solution of copper(II) sulphate to find the formula of the complex.

Investigation
relates to
Practical 13

Before you start, you must:
• carry out a risk assessment,
• discuss your plans with your teacher.

Investigations

Longer Investigations

L1 Do iron tables deteriorate?

Iron(II) compounds are slowly oxidised in air to iron(III) compounds, usually iron(III) oxide, Fe_2O_3. This compound, which is a brown, rusty colour, is insoluble in water and poorly absorbed from the stomach into the bloodstream.

Investigate whether the iron(II) sulphate in iron tablets gets significantly oxidised under various conditions. You could investigate factors such as:

- whether the tablets are whole or crushed,
- the presence of water,
- pH,
- temperature.

Do your answers suggest that deterioration by oxidation is likely to be a significant problem for the manufacturers and users of iron tablets?

relates to Practical 3

Before you start, you must:
- carry out a risk assessment,
- discuss your plans with your teacher.

L2 Looking at indicators from plants

Many plants contain dyes which are acid–base indicators. Red cabbage, beetroot and blackcurrant are examples. These indicators can be extracted by grinding the plant material with water or an organic solvent.

Investigate the indicators from a coloured plant of your choice. You could investigate:

- what colour the indicator is at different pH values,
- whether the indicator is a single dye, or a mixture,
- the acid–base strength of the indicator (see experiment 4 in Practical 10),
- whether different plants of the same colour contain the same indicator(s),
- whether different dyes can be combined to produce a type of universal indicator.

relates to Practical 10

Before you start, you must:
- carry out a risk assessment,
- discuss your plans with your teacher.

L3 Electrolysis of salt solution

The electrolysis of sodium chloride solution is an important source of industrial chemicals (*Chemistry in Context*, Fifth Edition, section 16.3). When concentrated sodium chloride solution is electrolysed, hydrogen is formed at the cathode and chlorine at the anode, with a solution of sodium hydroxide remaining. However, when the sodium chloride solution is very dilute, *oxygen* is formed at the anode instead of chlorine. What do you think happens with sodium chloride solution of intermediate concentration?

Investigate how the products at the anode are affected by the concentration of sodium chloride. Your investigation should be as quantitative as possible. You will need to think carefully about how you will collect and analyse the anode products and how you will deal with the toxic gas chlorine. You may need some guidance from your teacher on this.

relates to
Practical 21

Before you start, you must:
• carry out a risk assessment,
• discuss your plans with your teacher.

L4 The esterification equilibrium

Practical 14 gives a method you can use to find the equilibrium constant for the esterification reaction:

$$CH_3COOH + CH_3CH_2OH_2 \rightarrow CH_3COOCH_2CH_3 + H_2O$$

ethanoic acid   ethanol   ethyl ethanoate

Investigate the equilibrium further. You might investigate one or more of the following:

• the effect of temperature on the value of the equilibrium constant,
• the effect on the equilibrium constant of varying the concentration of catalyst,
• the rate at which equilibrium is reached.

relates to
Practical 14

Before you start, you must:
• carry out a risk assessment,
• discuss your plans with your teacher.

*It will be important to distinguish between the **position** of equilibrium and the **rate of attainment** of equilibrium. For example, varying the temperature will affect not only the value of the equilibrium constant, but also the rate at which equilibrium is reached. You will need to be satisfied that the reaction has had time to reach equilibrium before you make any measurements.*

L5 Investigating the formula of hydroxide precipitates

When sodium hydroxide solution is added to copper sulphate solution, a blue precipitate is formed. If, however, you do it the other way round and add the copper sulphate solution to the sodium hydroxide solution, you get a precipitate which is a different shade of blue and has a different formula.

Investigate the formulae of the precipitates. You might investigate one or more of the following questions.

• What is the formula of the precipitate formed when copper sulphate solution is added to sodium hydroxide solution, and vice versa?
• Do solutions of other copper salts behave in the same way?
• Do the salts of other metals show similar behaviour?

relates to
Practicals 23
and 24

Before you start, you must:
• carry out a risk assessment,
• discuss your plans with your teacher.

You will need to plan a way to find the formula of the precipitate. One possibility is to monitor the change in pH or conductivity as the solutions are added to one another.

L6 Comparing different methods of analysing for copper

Experiment 2 in Practical 4 shows how you can use an iodine/thiosulphate titration to find the concentration of copper(II) ions in a solution. This is only one of several methods you can use to analyse for copper.

Make up your own solution of copper(II) sulphate and use some of the following methods to find out the concentration of copper(II) ions.

- Weighing metallic copper displaced by zinc powder.

- Using a colorimeter.

- Using an edta titration.

- Adding a cation exchange resin and titrating the resulting solution with sodium hydroxide solution.

- Using an electrochemical cell.

You should be able to evaluate the effectiveness of the different techniques. Would they all be suitable for finding the percentage of copper in brass?

Investigation
relates to
Practical 4

> **Before you start, you must:**
> - carry out a risk assessment,
> - discuss your plans with your teacher.

L7 The kinetics of the peroxodisulphate/iodine reaction

Practical 15 gives a method for finding the order of a reaction by measuring the time taken for iodine to be formed. You can use the same idea to investigate the kinetics of the reaction between peroxodisulphate and iodide ions.

$$S_2O_8^{2-}(aq) + 2I^-(aq) \rightarrow 2SO_4^{2-}(aq) + I_2(aq)$$

In Practical 15 you have a single reaction mixture to which you keep adding sodium thiosulphate solution. You can adapt this method by designing a method in which you mix different volumes of peroxodisulphate and iodide ion solutions with a fixed volume of sodium thiosulphate solution.

You will have to think about what to change and what to keep constant in different experiments and how you can use your results to find the order of reaction with respect to peroxodisulphate and iodide ions.

You can also use your new method to investigate how the reaction rate is affected by temperature and so find a value for the activation energy. Practical 18 might help you formulate your plan.

You could extend your investigation still further to explore the effects of catalysts such as $Fe^{2+}(aq)$, $Fe^{3+}(aq)$ and other transition metal ions.

Investigation
relates to
Practicals 15
and 18

> **Before you start, you must:**
> - carry out a risk assessment,
> - discuss your plans with your teacher.

L8 The kinetics of the propanone/iodine reaction

Practical 17 uses a colorimeter to investigate the kinetics of a reaction in which a coloured reactant (bromine) is used up. You can use the same idea to investigate the kinetics of the reaction between propanone and iodine in acid solution.

$$CH_3COCH_3(aq) + I_2(aq) \rightarrow CH_3COCH_2I(aq)$$
$$+ H^+(aq) + I^-(aq)$$

By changing the composition of your mixture you can investigate:

- the order of reaction with respect to propanone,
- the order of reaction with respect to iodine,
- the order of reaction with respect to hydrogen ions.

relates to
Practicals 17
and 18

You will need to think carefully about what to change and what to keep constant in different experiments.

You can also investigate this reaction by stopping or 'quenching' it by running reaction mixtures into sodium carbonate solution at different times after mixing. You can then do a titration to find the concentration of the remaining iodine.

You can extend this procedure to investigate how the reaction rate is affected by temperature and so find a value for the activation energy. Practical 18 will help you formulate your plan.

Before you start, you must:
- carry out a risk assessment,
- discuss your plans with your teacher.

L9 How fast are dyes?

Two important features of dyes are the colour they impart to fabrics and their 'fastness'. Fastness is a measure of how strongly the dye is attached to the fabric. It is important in deciding whether the dye will 'run', in other words be lost into water when the material is washed.

Design a method to investigate the relative fastness to washing of different dyes used for fabrics such as wool or cotton. You could investigate dyes obtained from plants such as onions, red cabbage or stinging nettles. You may find that a colorimeter will allow you to be more precise in your measurements.

Sometimes fabrics are soaked in solutions of metal salts called mordants before dyeing to improve the fastness of the dye. You can investigate how effective mordants are. Some mordants change the colour of the dyed fabric. You can investigate this too.

Before you start, you must:
- carry out a risk assessment,
- discuss your plans with your teacher.

L10 The hydrolysis of bromobutane

1-Bromobutane is slowly hydrolysed to form butan-1-ol.

$$CH_3CH_2CH_2CH_2Br(l) + H_2O(l) \rightarrow$$
1-bromobutane

$$CH_3CH_2CH_2CH_2OH(aq) + H^+(aq) + Br^-(aq)$$
butan-1-ol

Investigate the factors which might affect the rate at which this reaction occurs. You might investigate one or more of the following:

- temperature,
- pH,
- the extent to which the 1-bromobutane is mixed with the aqueous phase.

Investigation

relates to
Practicals 28
and 29

Experiment 1 in Practical 28 might help you think of a way in which you can follow the rate of the reaction.

You could extend or modify this investigation in a number of ways.

- Look at different halogenoalkanes, containing different halogens and/or different alkanes.
- Look at different techniques for following the rate of the reaction, for example, using conductivity measurement. Your teacher may be able to suggest references.

Before you start, you must:
- carry out a risk assessment,
- discuss your plans with your teacher.